200 TIPS FOR
DE-CLUTTERING

200 TIPS FOR
DE-CLUTTERING

ROOM BY ROOM, including
OUTDOOR SPACES and
ECO TIPS

Daniela Santos Quartino

FIREFLY BOOKS

A FIREFLY BOOK

Published by Firefly Books Ltd. 2010

First printing

Publisher Cataloging-in-Publication Data (U.S.)

Quartino, Daniela Santos.
  200 tips for de-cluttering : room by room, including outdoor spaces and eco tips / Daniela Santos Quartino.
[800] p. : ill., col. photos. ; cm.
Summary: This book underlines the relationship between Feng Shui and de-cluttering. It provides tips on getting rid of clutter and achieving joy and balance.
ISBN-13: 978-1-55407-762-5
ISBN-10: 1-554007-762-1
1. Storage in the home. 2. Organization. 3. Orderliness. 4. Feng shui in interior decoration. I. Title.
648/.8 dc22   TX309.Q378   2010

Library and Archives Canada Cataloguing in Publication

Santos Quartino, Daniela
  200 tips for decluttering : room by room, including outdoor spaces and eco tips / Daniela Santos Quartino.
ISBN-13: 978-1-55407-762-5
ISBN-10: 1-554007-762-1
  1. House cleaning. 2. Orderliness. 3. Storage in the home.
I. Title. II. Title: two hundred tips for decluttering.
TX324.S25 2010   648'.5   C2010-901214-3

Published in the United States by
Firefly Books (U.S.) Inc.
P.O. Box 1338, Ellicott Station
Buffalo, New York 14205

Published in Canada by
Firefly Books Ltd.
66 Leek Crescent
Richmond Hill, Ontario L4B 1H1

Developed by LOFT Publications S.L.
Via Laietana, 32, 4th floor, office 92
08003 Barcelona, Spain
Ph: +34 93 268 8088
Fax: +34 93 268 7073
loft@loftpublications.com
www.loftpublications.com

For Loft:
Editor: Daniela Santos Quartino
Editorial Coordinator: Simone K. Schleifer
Assistant to Editorial Coordinator: Aitana Lleonart
Art Director: Mireia Casanovas Soley
Design and Layout Coordinator: Claudia Martínez Alonso
Layout: Cristina Simó

Cover design: Jacqueline Hope Raynor

Printed in China

INTRODUCTION

Your home is the epitome of your personality. Its appearance affects your mood and how you live. Its appearance is also fundamental to good health and to happy family relationships. Having "a place for everything" is also a time-saver. We tend to accumulate clothes, knick-knacks, books, furniture and a whole range of appliances over the years. The important thing is to avoid hoarding to the point that you obstruct your household's movement. Instead, foster your home's dynamics and your family's comfort. One of the most important steps to achieving balance and well-being is to get rid of cumbersome accumulations of stuff.

Perhaps there is no miraculous solution to keeping everything in its place, but there is an array of solutions tailored to the needs of each person and family, which greatly facilitate the task of

organization. One of the most important things is to choose good storage options. Some of the inspiring ideas covered in this book include how to properly lay out furniture, using forgotten corners and attics, walls that conceal closets, shelves that reach to the ceiling and dual-use items.

The process must be methodical, working on one bedroom, one closet or one desk at a time. Start with the space that presents the most organizational problems — the space that gives you the greatest feeling of discomfort and powerlessness. Ask questions like "What would I save in this room if it was on fire?" Honest replies will help you get rid of many unused things. As the space is cleared you will notice that the physical, tangible effect changes your state of mind, and this will encourage you to clear out and organize other areas of your home.

Your success depends more on your good judgment than the size of your budget, and customized decoration is fundamental. Achieving an uncluttered space that still contains everything you need is interesting and challenging. We become sharper when faced with difficulties, and many classic and original ideas can make use of every last inch of your home and change the lives of its inhabitants.

This book explores several solutions for storage, the organization of space for different rooms of the house and organizing outdoor spaces. Each chapter is illustrated with photographs of homes and features an extensive selection of contemporary furniture that will be essential to achieving your organizational goals.

KITCHENS

SUB-ZERO WOLF

KITCHENS

The contemporary kitchen is a highly technical space, combining aesthetics and practicality like nowhere else in the house. Primarily, the different work areas must be highly functional; a well-designed kitchen saves time, making the work and subsequent tidying up and cleaning of the spaces easier. It must also incorporate numerous essential appliances: refrigerator, oven, stove, microwave, dishwasher, etc. They all have a specific function and position, which is often dictated by the structure of the space as well as the placement of water faucets and power outlets.

BERLONI CUCINE

BULTHAUP

1 Kitchen furniture manufacturers offer different products that perform a vast array of functions. Moreover, there are many cabinet and drawer organizers available, which offer increasingly imaginative solutions.

Cabinets located beneath a window cover the entire lower wall and provide ample storage space without reducing the amount of natural light in the room. White is also used in the unit that integrates the kitchen sink and the stovetops, enhancing the effect.

2

3

Alternating decorative elements with doors and exposed shelves brings a sense of visual lightness to the space while also hiding the less decorative pieces of cookware.

When your cabinets are not
spacious enough to store all your
dishes and utensils or you do not
want to clutter your walls with high
cabinets, use shelves, small ledges
and rails with hooks to keep your
countertop tidy and orderly.

4

Linear organization solutions
are perfect for limited spaces.
Cabinets, which may clutter the
area, are not required here, as
there is a large pantry area at the
back of the room.

5

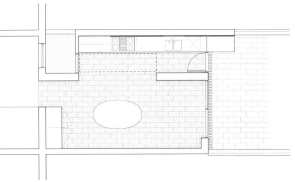

Heavier and more frequently used items, such as pots, pans, etc., should be stored in lower cabinets and deep drawers underneath the counter. Light and small items should be stored in higher wall cabinets or on exposed shelves and ledges, as you can easily store or access without them straining your back.

6

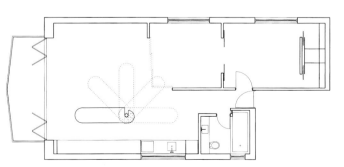

7

The lack of work space in this kitchen with clean and minimalist lines has been resolved with a revolving glass table, which can also be used as a dining table.

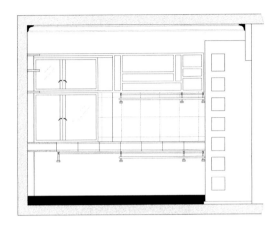

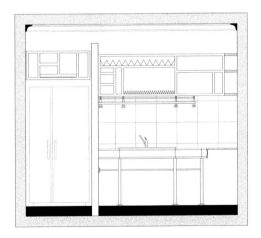

8

Maximum use of space has been achieved in this small U-shaped kitchen. To gain space, the cabinet doors have been removed.

9

A made-to-order wooden unit serves as a small but fully equipped kitchen — a perfect solution for small spaces, single-person households or where the kitchen is only used occasionally.

10

Exposed storage makes spaces look bigger, as the absence of doors visually lightens the area and provides easy access to all elements. Removing doors is an excellent option in small kitchens when you want to emphasize the feeling of spaciousness.

BERLONI CUCINE

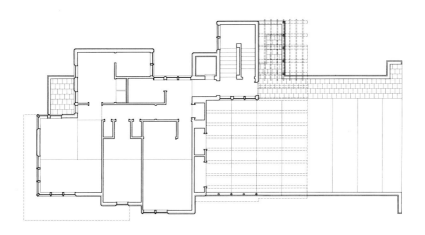

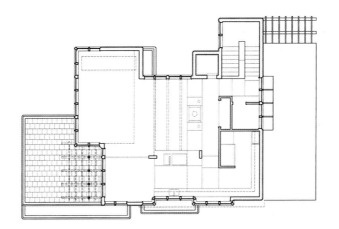

11   In an open-plan kitchen–living room, a low partition defines the spaces without separating the rooms. On the kitchen side, it serves as extra storage space to support low cabinets or small shelves, and the countertop can be used both as a breakfast bar and a work surface.

12 This living room and kitchen are separated by the two different heights of the island (which is also a breakfast bar) and the countertop. This solution also helps to partially hide the kitchen work surfaces.

BERLONI CUCINE

13

Cabinets that extend to the ceiling in columns are an ideal location for the refrigerator, oven and microwave, as well as a way to integrate pillars, setbacks or recesses into the wall. Avoid creating corners that are difficult to access, as they are dead spaces that will be tricky to keep tidy.

The wooden structure that organizes the two different heights of this house contains a fully equipped kitchen that fits perfectly into the narrow space. White lacquered cabinets provide the required storage.

ELMAR CUCINE

ELMAR CUCINE

14

When there is no space for a conventional dining table, a long floating counter adds a sense of lightness to a kitchen island and provides an extra work surface that can also be used as a breakfast bar.

Here, white has again been chosen to lacquer
high wall cabinets. The fact that the cabinets
only occupy part of the wall and do not have
handles contributes to the purity of the space.

This ingenious wall storage
system leaves the work surfaces
tidy. All utensils are within reach,
but they are hidden behind folding
doors and shutters.

15

BULTHAUP

There are many clever storage solutions for all kinds of kitchenware. For example, there are spice racks for all tastes and needs: wall racks, mini shelves, separate drawers or, the latest invention, jars "recessed" ad hoc into a wall.

16

BULTHAUP

17 Storage systems affixed to the wall keep countertops clear but still accommodate cooks who like to have everything within reach.

BULTHAUP

BULTHAUP

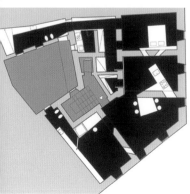

18

Specially made furniture makes full use of the potential of a space, even when the architectural structure is completely irregular. In addition, playing with volumes, materials and colors will add personality without clashing with the style of the home, creating a harmonious ensemble.

MOVE

>> 19 Rule number one in the kitchen is to keep everything near the area where it is used. For example, dishes and flatware near the everyday dining table, pots and pans next to the stove and seasonings, and condiments and utensils near the work surface.

DADA

DADA

>>20 The best storage solutions for kitchens are columns about 12 inches (80 cm) wide with individual compartments, removable baskets and shelves, as well as units with articulated or rotating trays and bottle compartments.

HABITAT

ARMANI/DADA

DADA

CESAR

>>21 Store your everday kitchen tools in drawers and on shelves that are hip height, so they are within easy reach and you don't need to bend over. Items that are used less frequently should be stored in lower drawers.

ARMANI/DADA

BOFFI

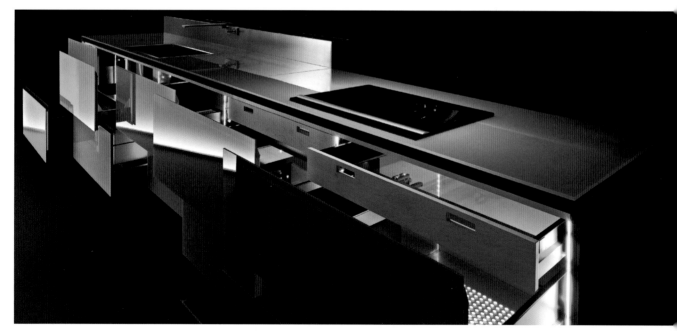

VALCUCINE

TECNOCUCINA

CESAR

ERNESTO MEDA

PEDINI

PORCELANOSA

>> 22 Double-height drawers can be used to store dishes and cookware. Integrate an internal drawer to hold flatware, napkins, coasters, tablecloths and the like.

CESAR

CHMIDT

>>23

Kitchen islands are ideal for large kitchens and will extend your work surface. They may also be used as a dining table, and you can integrate storage modules in them.

ARMANI/DADA

TECNOCUCINA

HABITAT

SCHIFFINI

CESAR

CESAR

>>24 A sliding cover for the sink maximizes space, serving as an extra work surface and hiding the sink when it is not in use.

CESAR

CNOCUCINA

TECNOCUCINA

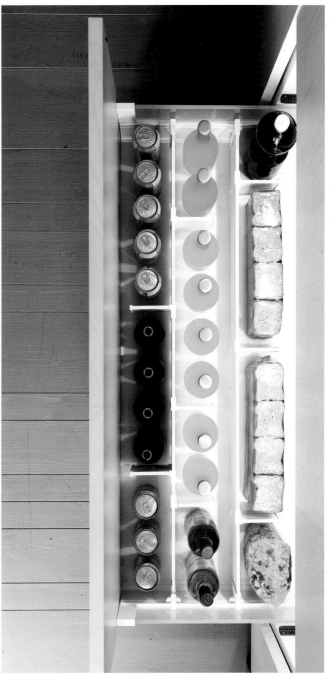

CESAR

SCHIFFINI

>> 25 Islands must have a minimum size of 3¼ to 4 feet (1 to 1.2 m) by 2¼ to 2½ feet (70 to 80 cm) so they are comfortable to work at and there is sufficient storage space. If the stovetop and sink are built into it, the measurements should be increased.

RATIONAL

ERNESTO MEDA

CESAR

DADA

CESAR

CESAR

CESAR

CESAR

ESAR

ESAR

DADA

ERNESTO MEDA   IKEA

ARDY INSIDE

IKEA

MOBALCO

TEKA

TEKA

ADA

TECNOCUCINA

DADA

RATIONAL

TING

DADA

DA

TECNOCUCINA

BITAT

>>26

Magnetic bars or rails on which to hang utensils allow you to have your most used utensils within reach and well organized. Place the bars and rails on the wall space between the countertop and the cabinets, and sort the objects according to type and use.

A

RMANN-COPENHAGEN

LA OCA

NORMANN-COPENHAGEN

IKEA

OMAD

HABITAT

ZANOTTA

ZANOTTA

ARTIFICIO

BOFFI

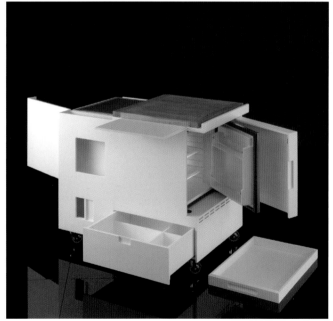

BOFFI

BOFFI

DORADA

O&G

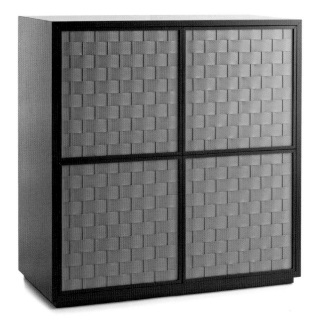

RASCHIN

HOME
OFFICES

NUEVA LÍNE

HOME OFFICES

More and more people are deciding to work from home. Hence the need to furnish a room or corner of the house with specific functions and organizational features. New technologies have profoundly changed the way people work and study: there are more cables and less bookshelves. The secret to maintaining order a work area is to assign a place for everything. What can be found easily can also be tidied up easily. If you think about what you use the item for it will help you store it in a logical place.

ANOTTA

27 Work stations can get very untidy, so a drawer, shelf or unit where all essential material is at hand but not in your way is a must. A work station on wheels is a good solution.

IMA MOBIL

Your way of working and organizing your space is something personal and subjective.
When workers share a space and use it at the same time, each must have their own desk for their belongings, where they can organize their work to their liking.

28

When space is limited, resources must be shared. Here, a shelf serves as a side desk, a bookcase and a shoe rack.

29

30

A low bookcase can separate spaces without dividing the room or obstructing light. This basic principle has been taken into account here, giving this work area a certain air of privacy.

O.T.S. SELL

ightly wider than normal shelf in a bookcase erfect for a place to write or to put a small puter. This solution is suitable when space mited and a large or demanding work area t required.

31

A work area can be arranged anywhere, but do not settle for just any corner if you would like a comfortable and efficient space. An option in smaller homes is to open up a closet and take advantage of the space by fitting two or three shelves and a desk inside.

DESAL

ESALTO

32   Visually, the lightest storage system is one attached to a wall, particularly if the shelves are made from metal or glass. There is a wide array of exclusive and original designs available.

The dimensions of bookshelves must be adapted to the available space and the intended use so you can work comfortably. Specially made units make the most of the space available and the height of the ceilings, and they can also adapt to recesses and projections in the wall.

33

WOG

MOLTENI

34

Modular furniture allows for multiple combinations and heights, and it can be further expanded. There are sizes and styles for all tastes on the market.

35

The open ceiling of this half-basement harnesses the light and vents the cluttered space below. The large bookcase integrates the desk on one side as well as the side desk underneath.

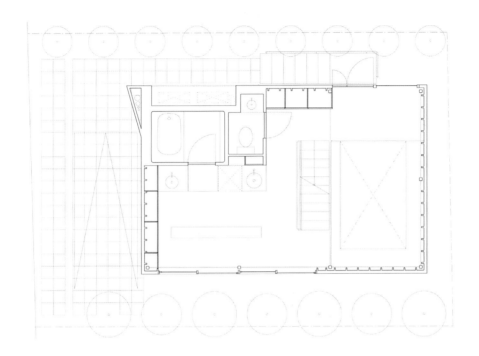

36   Tall bookcases to the ceiling are decorative and have great storage capacity, but you must optimize their use and make all corners accessible.

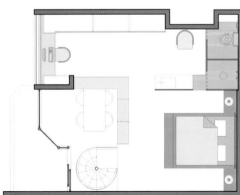

37 A well-distributed work area can integrate books and files on shelves and cabinets and share space with a closet, making the most of the space.

38

In general, the width of the shelf of a bookcase should be 10 to 12 inches (25 to 30 cm), or 15 to 20 inches (40 to 50 cm) if large-format books or bulky items are going to be stored, or roughly 6 inches (15 cm) if intended to hold CDs and DVDs. Using double-shelved units on wheels, which can be moved around, can significantly increase the storage capacity.

A light and pleasant atmosphere, even in a small space, always conveys a sense of order and tranquility and makes work a pleasant activity. It is unlikely that an area cluttered with furniture will look tidy.

39

40

Hiding the desk behind floor-to-ceiling panels made of wood or cloth — or just concealing part of a bookcase — integrates the work area into the space but ensures it will not interfere with the decor or disturb others when it is not in use, creating a multifunctional room.

ORRO

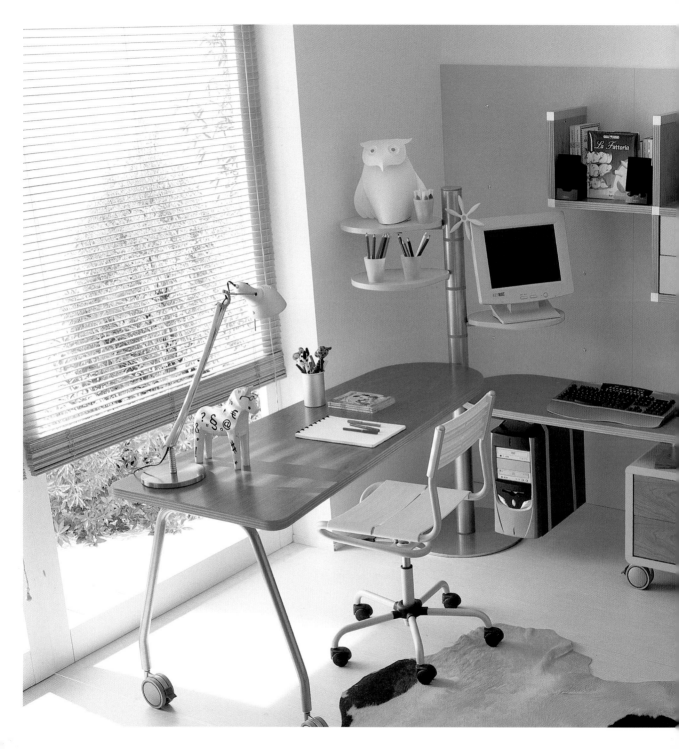

41

In confined spaces, a desk on wheels or one with an extra panel that can be folded out to create a larger work surface is a good idea, since when folded away it occupies minimal space.

DEAR KID

148

BONALDO

SANA

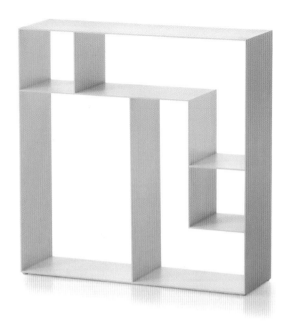

BUSNELLI

CAPELLINI

ARKETIPO

>>42 You may not need a desk for everyday use, you may want to conceal it if it does not have its own room, or you may not want it to form part of the decoration of your home's common areas. In these cases, furniture units with a built-in and concealable desk are ideal.

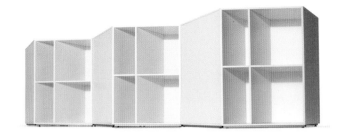

ARTFLEX

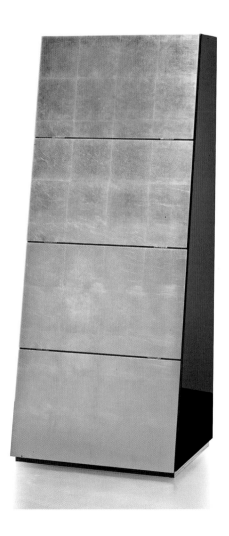

AB

WOGG

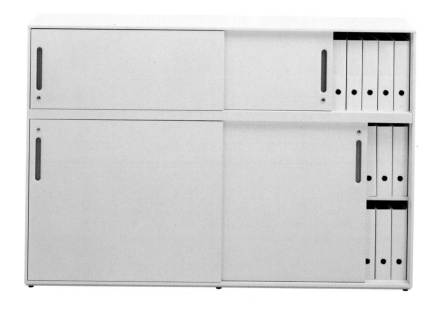

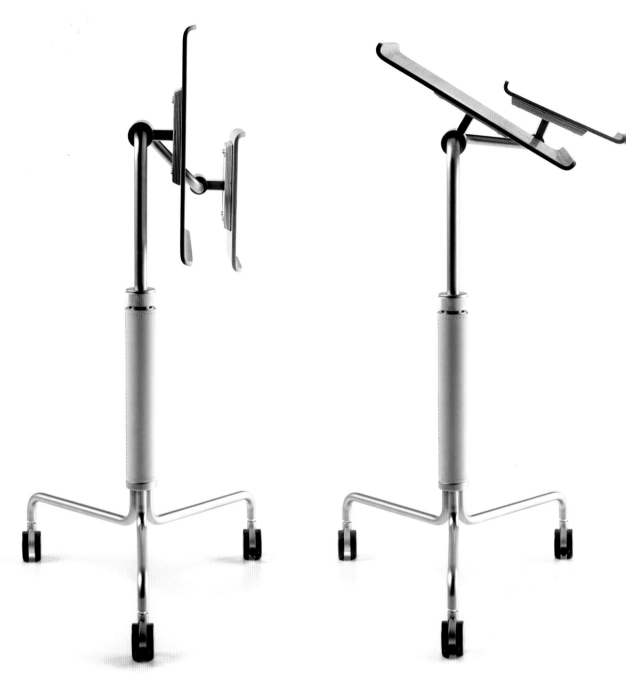

ARCHIMEDE

DESALTO

>>43 Light shelves are an ideal way to take advantage of setbacks in a wall and create built-in bookcases. Another way to enhance the sense of space is by affixing bookcases to a wall and leaving a space beneath for a computer desk or other pieces of furniture.

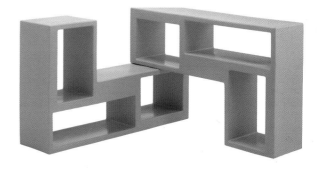

CASAMANIA

ALTO

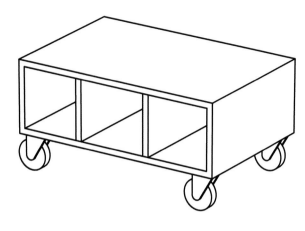
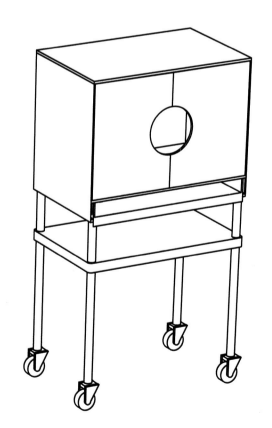

KABALAB

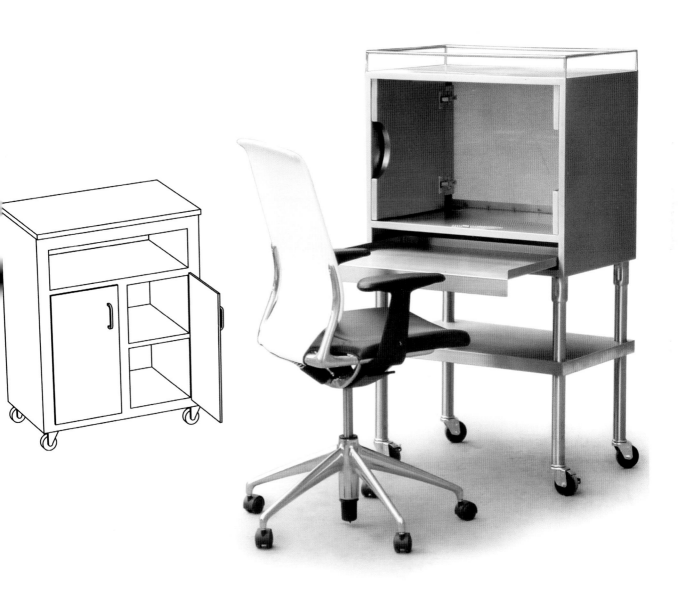

BALAB

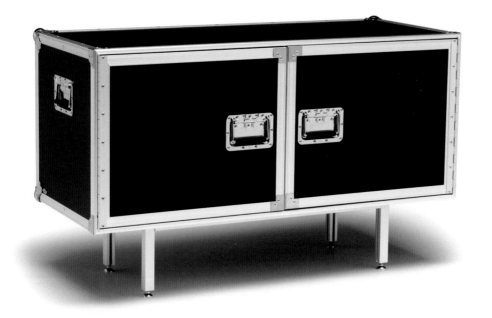

DIESEL BY MOROSO

ROCHE BOBOIS

FITTING

MUJI

GEL BRECHTS

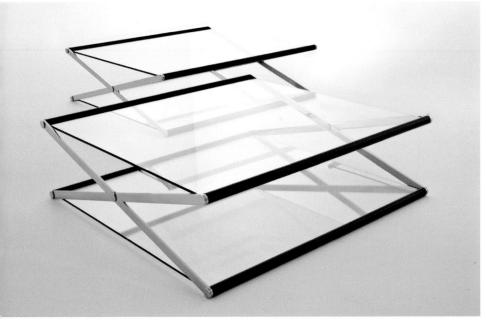

OTTI & RADICE

E15

GIORGETTI

LAURA MERONI

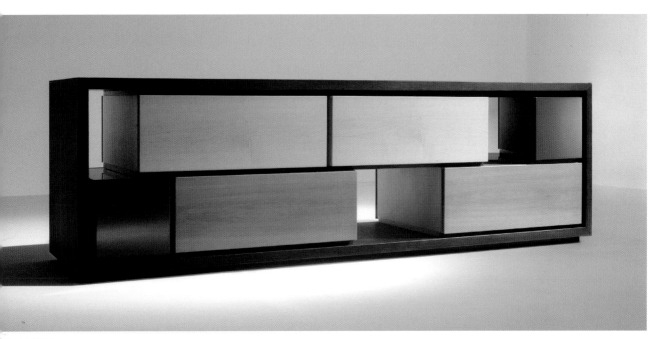

RA MERONI

F ITALIA

IKEA

LAURA MERONI

GIS

MDF ITALIA

F ITALIA

MUJI

MDF ITALIA

MINOTTI

>>**44** A bookcase is a good way to separate the work area from the rest of the room. If a cabinet has a back, apply wallpaper to bring a touch of color to the room.

PIANCA

DF ITALIA

MODÀ

MODÀ

172

ODÀ

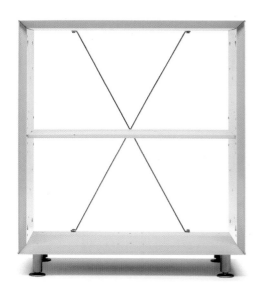

OBLES 114

ROCHE BOBOIS

MUJI

MOBLES 114

MUJI

MUJI

MUJI

MUJI

VICCARBE

>>**45** Creating a work area at the entrance of the house is an ideal way to make use of space that is often wasted. Simply place a narrow desk instead of an accent table near the entrance and add a small chest of drawers.

RÖ

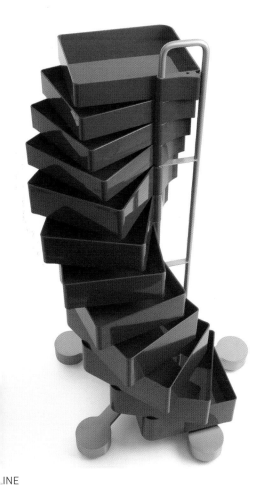

.INE

RÖ

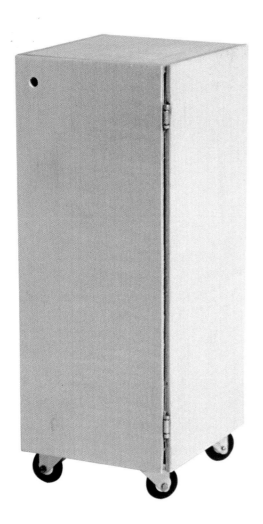

KABALAB

ROCHE BOBOIS

RÖ

MOBLES 114

CHE BOBOIS

ROCHE BOBOIS

DO+CE

EMMEMOBILI

NCA

>>46

When establishing the work area, the ideal setup includes a large table that offers enough space for a laptop, equipment, documents and materials.

NAN & ERWAN BOUROULLEC DESIGN

MISO SOUP DESIGN

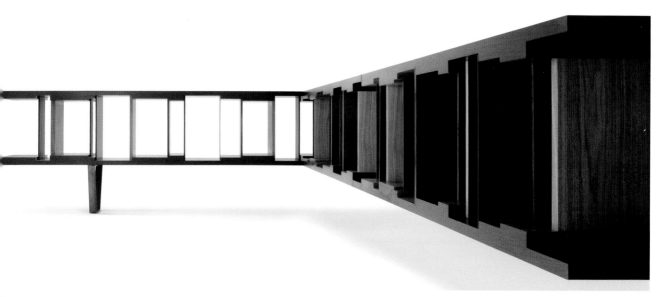

CCOTTI

HARD LAMPERT

B-LINE

VITRA

SEVENSALOTTI

NOTTA

BEDROOMS

BEDROOMS

The multifunctional and versatile common areas of a home do not eliminates the need to enjoy intimate spaces. The bedroom, which was traditionally only a room to sleep in, has become an individual living space where one studies, plays, reads, listens to music, etc. These multiple uses also require flexible design solutions so that new items, beyond clothing and bedding, have a place to be stored.

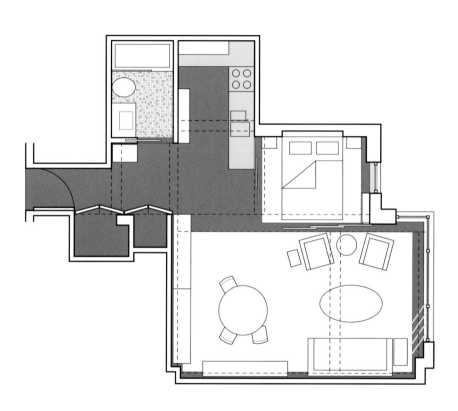

47

A ledge or recess in the headboard of the bed can be used to store personal items, photos or keepsakes in decorative boxes. If there is not enough space, a bedside table can also be used, which won't clutter the room.

Dividing the room by installing a freestanding closet will not necessarily make the room appear visually smaller. Fitting transparent or frosted glass doors or a mirror are options without any major drawbacks.

48

49

Painting or lacquering closet doors the same color as the walls visually integrates them into the room. It is best to use light colors, as this will minimize the visual impact of the furniture and visually widen the space.

50

A closet without doors is an option, and your clothes will be more accessible. However, everything must be perfectly organized. A bright and colorful painted or papered wall defines the space that the closet would have occupied, without the bulk of furniture.

MOVE

When storing less frequently used objects in a closet or dressing room, sort them by category and place them in boxes with lids (labeled if possible). The contents will be protected from dust, but you will be able to find whatever you're looking for quickly.

51

ELLIGOTTI

52 Freestanding closets are, in theory, unsuitable for small spaces because they visually invade much of the space; however, they offer more variety in terms of style, color and material.

53

In homes with different ceiling heights or sloping roofs, built-in or custom-built closets make the best use of the storage space available, maximizing awkward corners.

LEMA

Large and small chests of drawers are a must for storing delicate or smaller items — which should be organized in boxes — as they free up space in the closet for shelves and rods.

54

OLTENI

MOLTE

LEMA

55

If you would like to have a dressing room, ensure that it is large enough to be used comfortably once all the closets have been installed. If it is a long space, place a seat at the back of the room or, if it is more square shaped, in the middle, so you can dress and undress more comfortably.

MOLTE

Most beds with storage space under the mattress have a spring base. The advantages are the large storage capacity, the ease of access and the visibility of the contents.

56

NOTTA

57

A room free of nonessential elements is a haven for relaxation and rest. When separating spaces is complicated by a lack of space or funds, a good option is a simple curtain to hide the closet or bathroom.

BELLIGOTTI

58

If there is enough room, conceal the closet with a floor-to-ceiling sliding panel along the widest wall, which will separate the dressing area from the sleeping area and maximize storage space.

MOVE

MA

MOLTENI

MUEBLES BENICARLÓ

>>59 Closets must be combined with other pieces of furniture in the bedroom, such as a chest of drawers and bedside tables. If they are not all the same style, all pieces should at least be the same color.

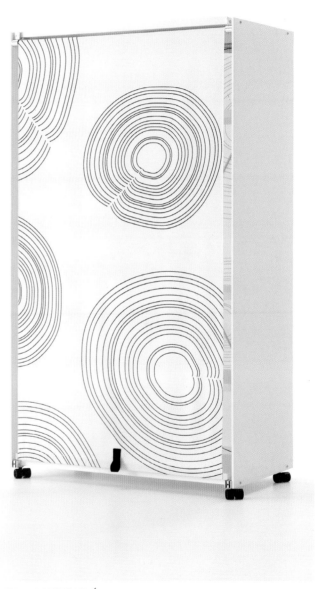

EBLES BENICARLÓ

MUEBLES BENICARLÓ

MUEBLES BENICARLÓ

CIA INTERNATIONAL

LA OCA

IKEA

Bedroom closets must be well organized so that you can find clothes, shoes an accessories easily. Specia rods, shelves and drawers play a key role.

IKEA

LEMA

EBI

FRATELLI SPINELLI

FRATELLI SPINELLI

FRATELLI SPINELLI

PORRO

>> 61

Getting rid of clothes that you no longer wear, avoiding the use of wire hangers (because they get tangled easily), hanging clothes by category, putting what you use least to the back of the closet and storing shoes on shelves are some basic points that will help you maintain order in closets.

PRESOTTO

PRESOTTO

PRESOTTO

PRESOTTO

MUJI

PRESOTTO

>>62

The bedside table is a classic piece of furniture, allowing you to organize reading material close to the bed, but it is not the only option. Books and magazines can be neatly stacked near the headboard without obstructing movement in the bedroom.

MUEBLES BENICARLÓ

CO MAT

DEESAWAT

DOMODINAMICA

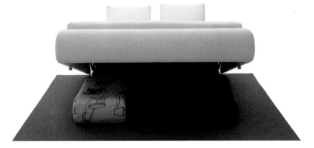

MPEGGI

CO MAT

>>**63** Today, a wide range of resources that make use of every square foot of a home are available. The use of convertible furniture is one of the best and easiest ways to keep small rooms tidy.

CAMPEGGI

LA CUCINA DI SARA

CAMPEGGI

EMMEMOBILI

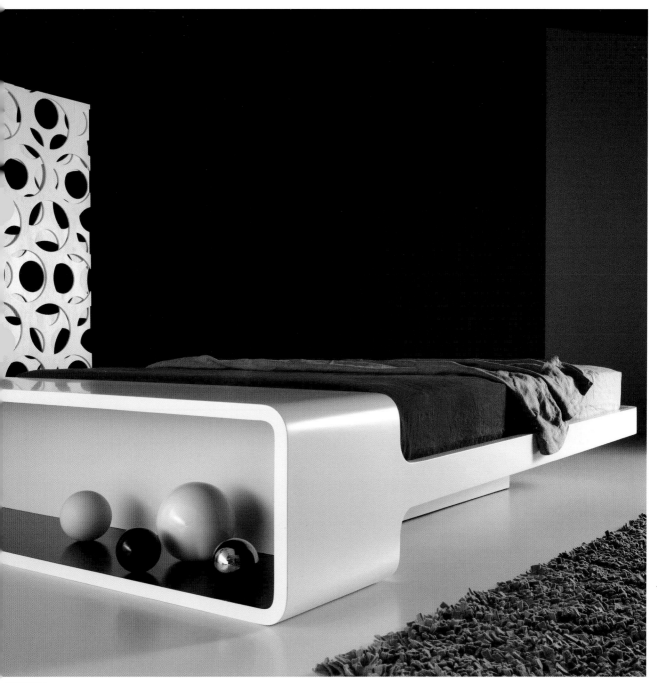

FRATELLI SPINELLI

TELLI SPINELLI

CAMPEGGI

MILANO BEDDING

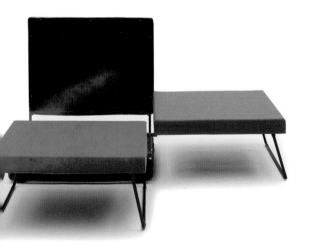

MPEGGI

EMMEMOBILI

IVIERI

ROCHE BOBOIS

ROCHE BOBOIS

ROCHE BOBOIS

WOGG

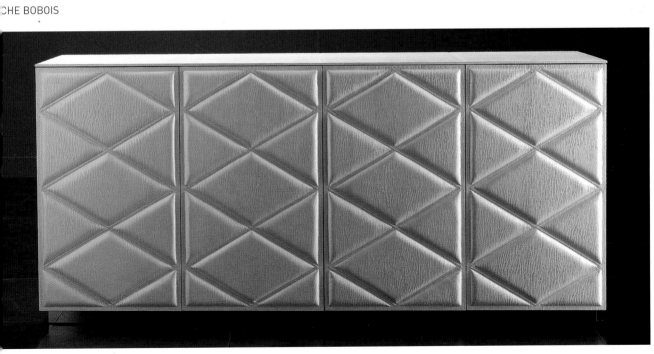

FORMER

>>64 Space under the bed should not be wasted. If the bed does not have any built-in shelving, there are a wide range of large-capacity flat boxes in which you can store anything, from shoes to sheets and blankets.

FLOU

EMMEMOBILI

ART BEDS

SMART BEDS

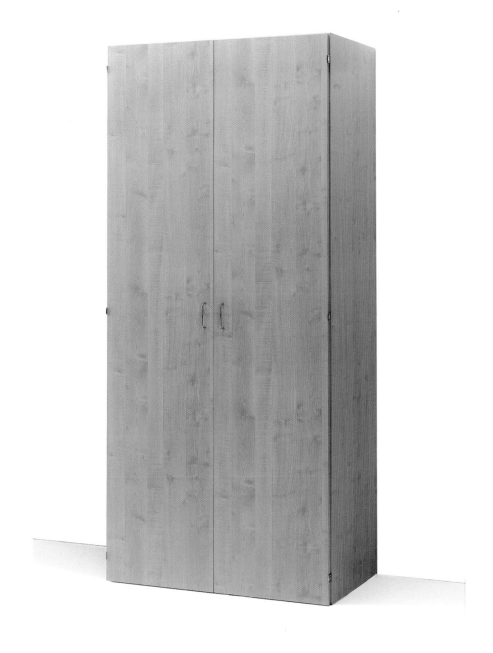

RT BEDS

SMART BEDS

Trundle beds are ideal for children's rooms, home offices or guest bedrooms. They can be used as an extra bed for guests without taking up too much space.

ART BEDS

COCO MAT

SMART BEDS

IKEA

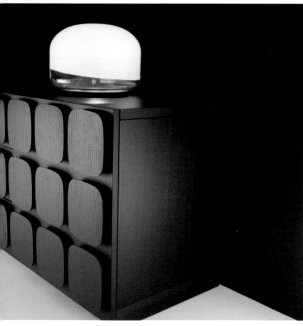

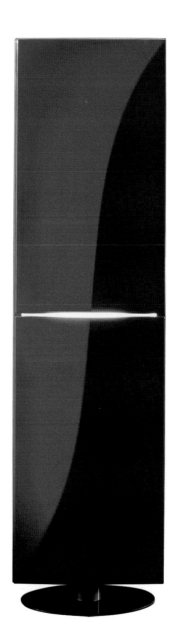

EMOBILI

ROCHE BOBOIS

MUEBLES BENICARLÓ

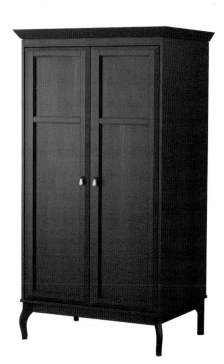

IKEA

>> **66** If there are no built-in closets, use freestanding units that suit your needs. It is better if they can be moved easily and organized into several different storage combinations.

ROCHE BOBOIS

RÖ

RÖ

RGETTI

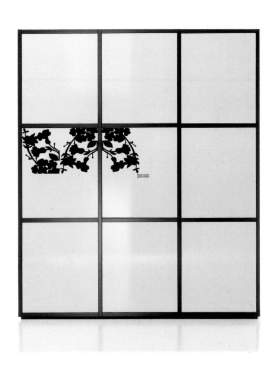

DÀ

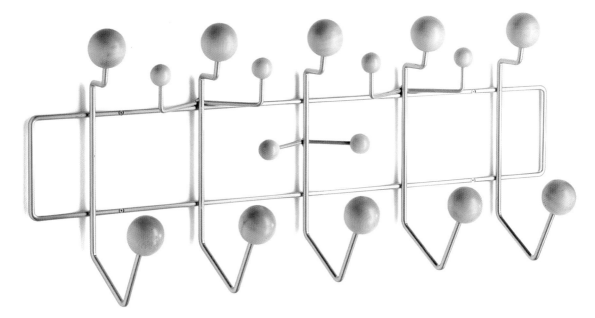

SMART BEDS

FLOU

BO CONCEPT

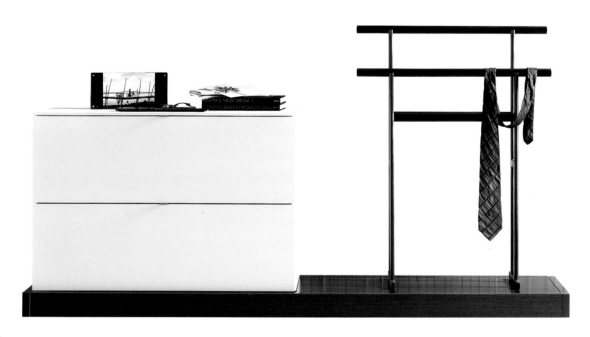

LA OCA

KTJOHANSER

MDF ITALIA

GNUS LONG

SANKTJOHANSER

FORMER

FFY LONDON

MOLTENI

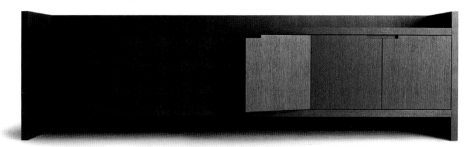

MEMOBILI

MODÀ

ROBOTS

>>67 You can transform a room in your home into a dressing room. This will solve all your clothing and footwear storage problems. To take full advantage of this space, it is important that you plan it carfully, making use of every last corner and, if necessary, customizing pieces of furniture.

PRESOTTO

HARD LAMPERT

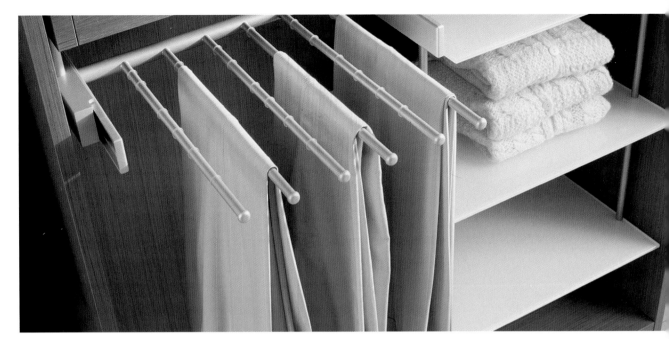

MOVE

MOVE

WOGG

KIDS' ROOMS

KIDS' ROOMS

Imagination and flexibility are the two basic ingredients for planning, furnishing and decorating a children's space. Imagination to equal a child's overflowing abundance of creativity, and flexibility to adapt to changes that occur at a speed that would certainly be a nightmare for even an experienced interior designer. This section, based on the latest trends in decorating children's spaces, is intended to be a useful guide for any parent interested in planning and decorating their child's bedroom or any other space where a child might spend time on a daily basis.

OMOBILI

68

Furniture on wheels or tracks allows you to change the layout of the elements in the room depending on the use required at any given time.

DEAR KIDS

69

A chest at the foot of the bed, as well being a large container, makes dressing and undressing easier for small children.

A chest with a hinged lid can be used as a seat or a side table with the benefit of added storage. In children's bedrooms, it can also be used as a toy chest.

70

BA MOBILI

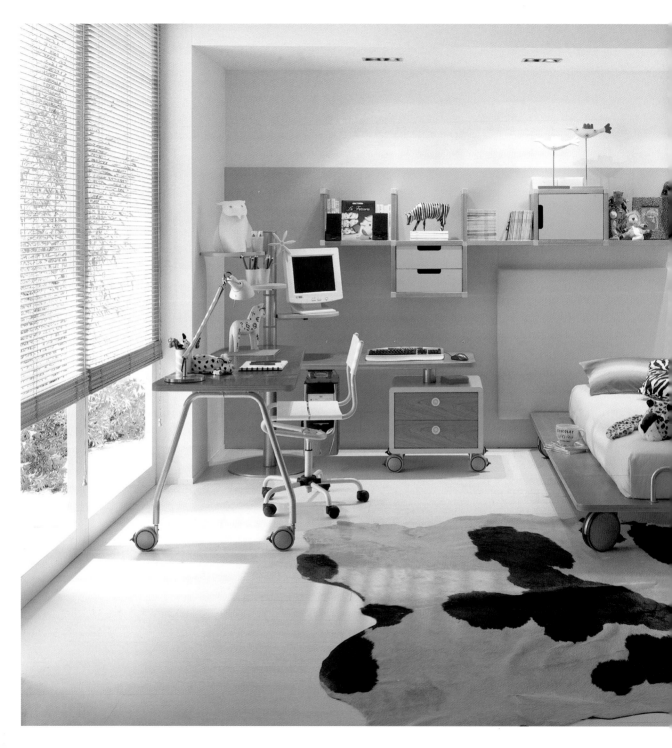

71

Color is a resource that can be used to create a sense of order and visually unify the numerous elements in the room.

DEAR KIDS

IMA MOB

72

Small cabinets placed halfway up a wall can be used as both a shelf and a base for a coat rack.

73

In just 22 square feet (2 m²), this space houses both the study and sleeping areas with a structure that incorporates both the desk and the bed. A ladder provides access to the upper level.

74

Good use has been made of this awkward space, with shelves, closets, drawers and a table and seat, which fit perfectly into the structure and can be neatly stored when not in use.

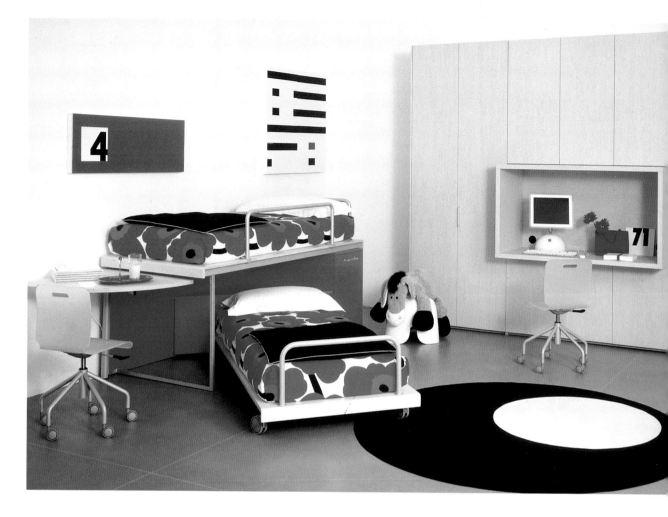

Units that can be transformed in order to provide several functions are the perfect way to make the most of small rooms or to create rooms that might not be used as often, such as a guest room.

75

341

Pieces that have several functions, such as this crib/changing table/ dresser, are not only ideal for small spaces but also make caring for infants easier.

76

77

Labeled baskets, boxes on wheels
that can be hidden under a bench
and a play area under the bed that
can be hidden behind a curtain are
solutions that make a space
easier to tidy up.

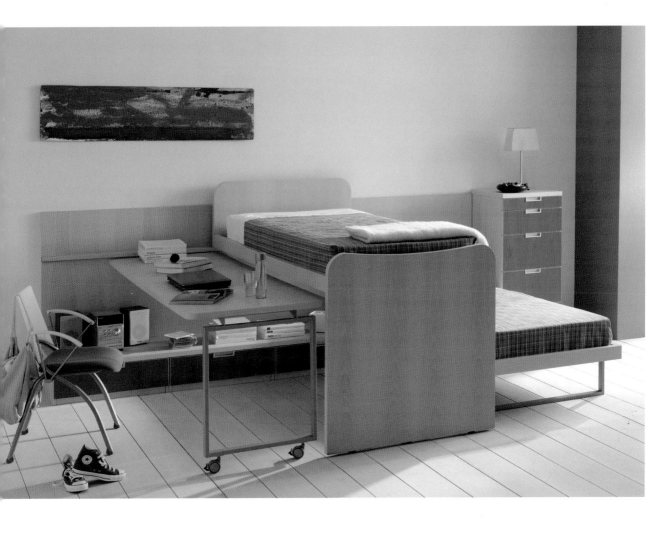

KIDS' ROOM FURNITURE

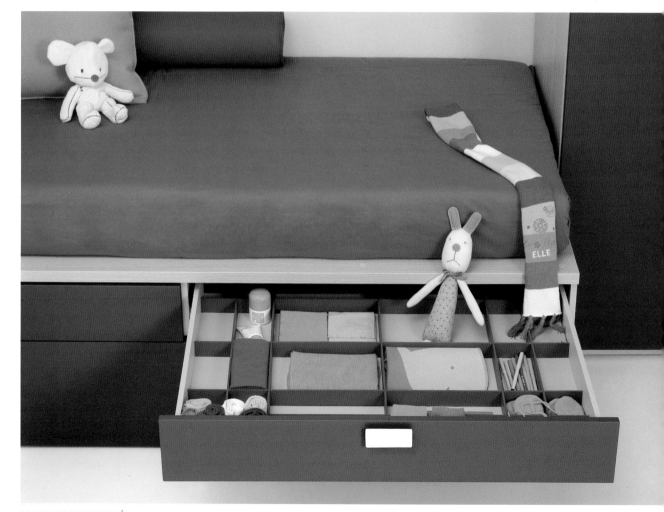

MUEBLES BENICARLÓ

>> **78** Markers, crayons and many small toys can get into every nook and cranny of the house. If they are stored in drawers—if possible drawers with internal organizers—it is easier to keep them in order.

R KIDS   IKEA

MUEBLES BENICARLÓ

DDO & PEREGO

MUEBLES BENICARLÓ

MUEBLES BENICARLÓ

BLES BENICARLÓ

MUEBLES BENICARLÓ

BLES BENICARLÓ

>> **79** Colorful furniture with classic lines, and without childish drawings or decorations, will stand the test of time and last until the child becomes a teenager or even a young adult eliminating the need to change the main furniture in the bedroom.

MUEBLES BENICARLÓ

DEAR KIDS

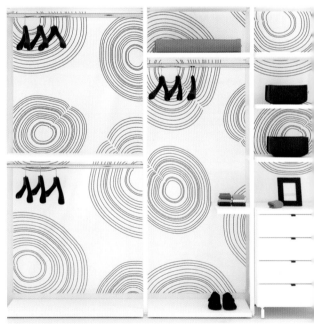

MUEBLES BENICARLÓ

EBI

MUEBLES BENICARLÓ

BLES BENICARLÓ

MUEBLES BENICARLÓ

EMMEMOBILI

MUEBLES BENICARLÓ

EMMEBI

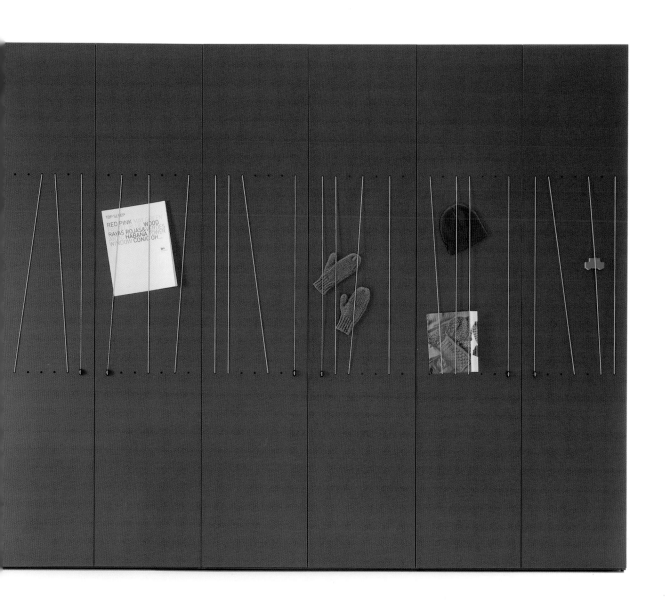

Decorating a teenager's
bedroom with reproductions
of artwork is a good idea, as
it will increase their interest
in art. The closet door is ideal
for this type of decoration.

CIA INTERNATIONAL

KIDS

DI LIDDO & PEREGO

ES BENICARLÓ

MUEBLES BENICARLÓ

ES BENICARLÓ

MUEBLES BENICARLÓ

>>**81** The units below include all the essential furniture and frames the bed between shelves, drawers and cabinets. It saves space and provides extra storage. If a trundle bed is used, have spare bed beneath for a sibling or friend.

MUEBLES BENICARLÓ

MUEBLES BENICARLÓ

FITTING

DEAR KIDS

MUEBLES BENICARLÓ

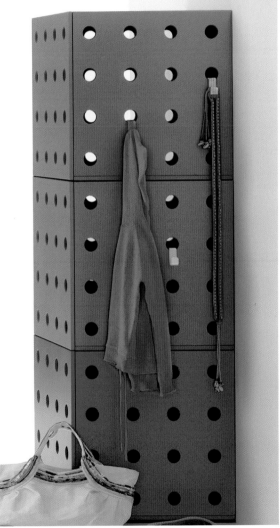

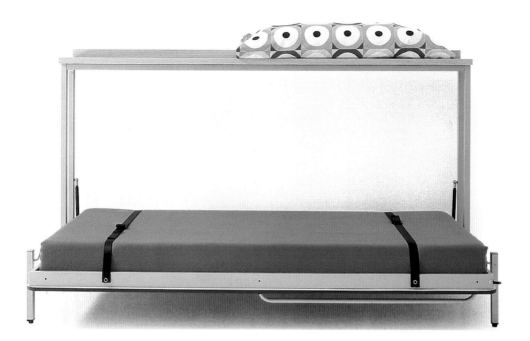

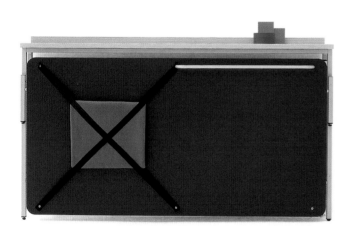

MUEBLES BENICARLÓ

IKEA

DEAR KIDS

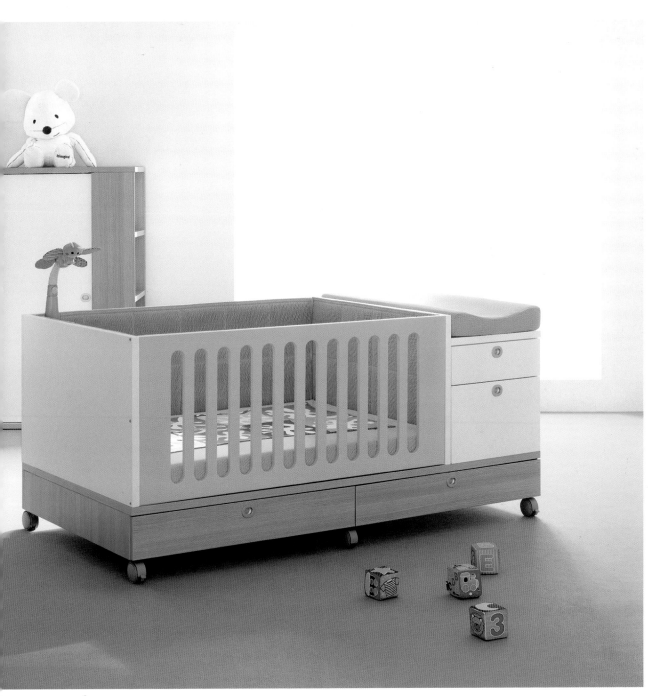

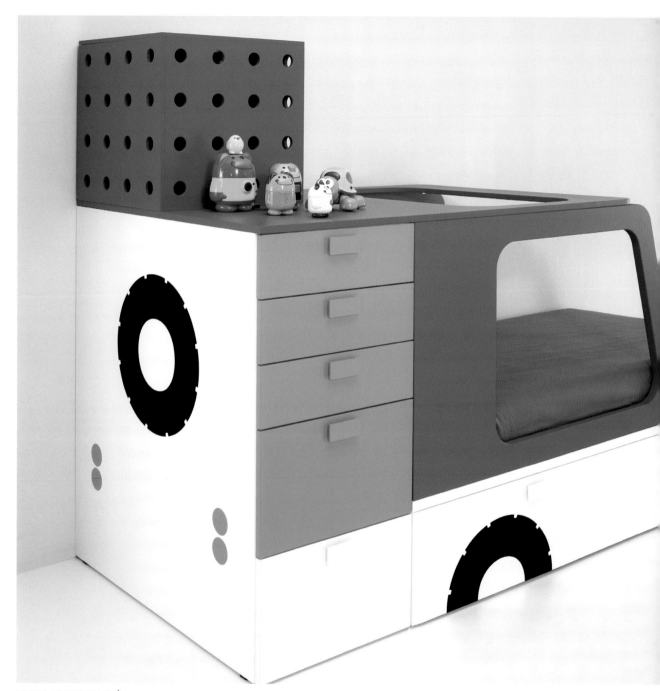

MUEBLES BENICARLÓ

MUEBLES BENICARLÓ

MUEBLES BENICARLÓ

P'KOLINO

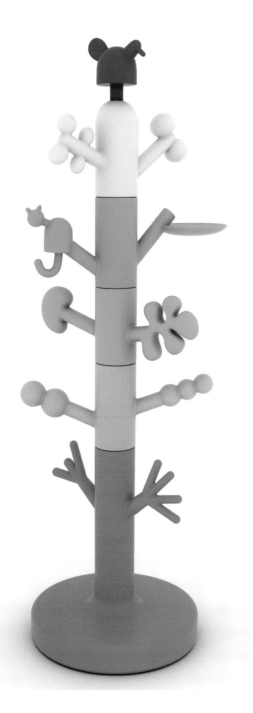

S

P'KOLINO

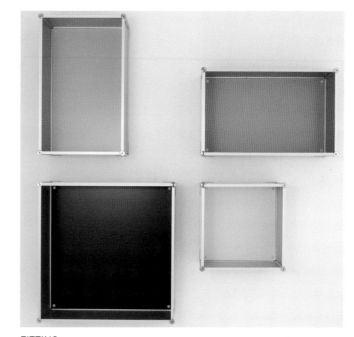

FITTING

MUEBLES BENICARLÓ

82

The easier it is for childre
to put away their toys
themselves, the longer th
bedroom will remain tidy.
Furniture or boxes withou
lids are ideal.

MUEBLES BENICARLÓ

MUEBLES BENICARLÓ

CIA INTERNATIONAL

JOE PIPAL

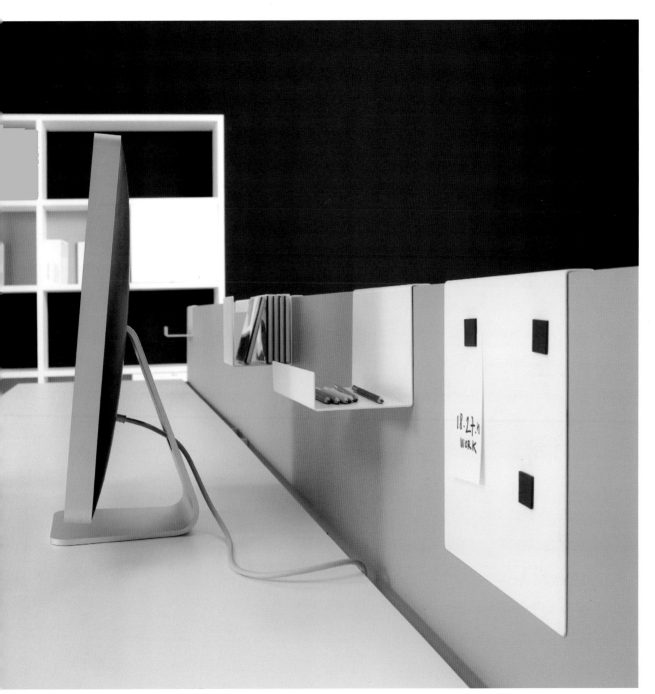

18.27.4
WORK

DEAR KIDS

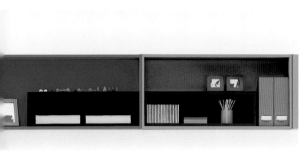

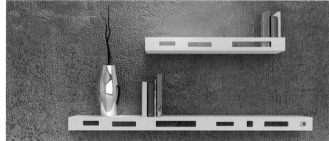

IKEA

ES BENICARLÓ

HALLWAYS &
PASSAGES

HALLWAYS & PASSAGES

Hallways are, in most cases, gold mines of space that should be exploited for greater storage capacity in contemporary homes. Foyers, staircases and landings are the forgotten spaces of interior design, yet they structure the space and often determine the organization of the rooms, giving coherence to the whole house. These spaces may offer versatile and functional storage solutions, with shelves, hangers, small closets and medium-sized furniture that can be used and shared by the occupants of the house.

83

Installing closets along walls is the best solution, clearing the view of objects and creating a lot of storage. These closets must be integrated into the architecture. This solution is only suitable for large walls.

PORRO

Stairwells offer a wide range of
useful possibilities, from a rod to
hang up coats on to a space for a
chest of drawers, a sofa bed or an
inconspicuous closet system.

84

Blurring the boundaries between rooms lets you gain depth and space. In the passage between this entrance and lounge, there is a ledge with a music system.

85

86 Playing with colors and materials can emphasize storage systems if you want them to stand out, for example, in an entrance hall, or hide them in order to aesthetically standardize the space and make it seem visually larger, as in a hallway or stairwell.

87 Landings can be maximized by installing a narrow shelf for books, CDs, trinkets or shoes.

In buildings with many levels, use the staircases as bookcases which can adapt to the continual changes in the architectural structure, converting these passageways into a reflection of your lifestyle.

88

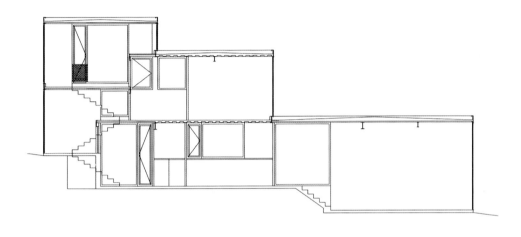

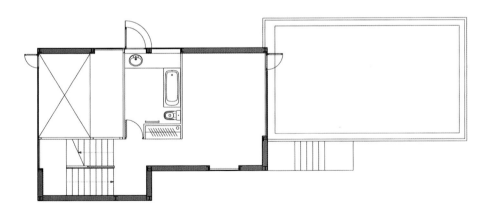

Elements that define rooms,
such as doors, steps, structural
columns, beams and shelves,
offer corners in which to
assemble free standing or
built-in cabinets and shelving.

89

90 High ceilings are a great resource. If they are high enough you can construct an attic, for storage, or a false ceiling, which provides storage capacity similar to that of a closet.

In this narrow house, all partitions have been removed. Everything is integrated into one space, with a large closet covering the entire wall and providing the required storage space.

91

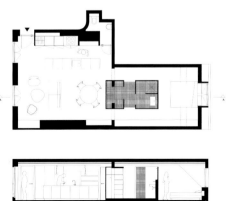

92

A custom-built bookshelf that runs along the entire wall of an apartment gives the space a certain stylish continuity, but it does not necessarily need to be uniform. Playing with different heights can alter and differentiate the space.

A wall cabinet at a medium to low height in a hallway or foyer provides a useful surface on which to place small decorative items, a phone or a coin tray, as well as serving as a shelf at the entrance to the home.

93

94 A closet covered in the same material as an adjacent pillar or freestanding column integrates the structural elements of the architecture and decor and defines the area.

Here, the structure of the
staircase is used for shelves at
varying heights, which are made
from the same material as the
wall on which they are installed.

95

A bookcase in a hallway is a typical solution to maximize wall space, although it is better to leave a space between it and the ceiling, for accessibility and to avoid cluttering the space. The hallway must be at least 3 feet (1 m) wide to be able to move comfortably through it.

96

Gain a library by refurbishing a balcony. When interior space is scarce, renovating part of the house's outside space to obtain the required additional surface area can be a good solution.

97

98

If the kitchen is too small to hold all the essentials needed to work comfortably, they must be placed elsewhere in the home. The important elements that can usually be located outside the kitchen are shelves, the pantry and the refrigerator.

MOL

Occasional furniture, such as a chest of drawers or an accent table, are available in a wide range of styles and designs, making them very versatile for spaces such as entrances, living rooms, family rooms and dining rooms.

99

ELAN ITALIA

100

A chest of drawers in the hallway offers extra storage space for items that are only occasionally used but essential in a home: spare lightbulbs, batteries, candles, cell phone charger, etc.

The different levels of this house
are connected by modules and
structures, which are perfect places
for a couple of shelves or cabinets.

101

If it is not possible to install a built-in closet near the entrance, a small freestanding closet in the entrance or at the back of the hallway is the perfect place to store coats, bags and hats.

102

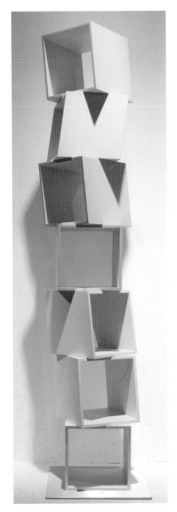

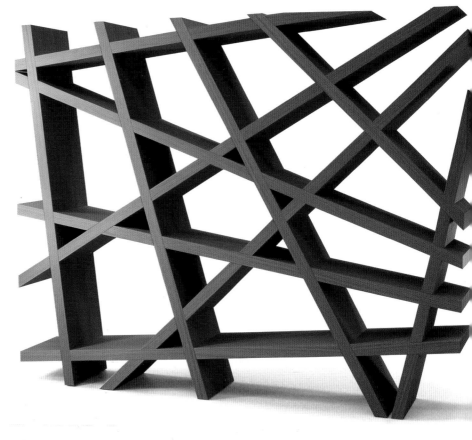

EMMEBI

EMMEMOBILI

>> **103** There is little space for shelves in narrow hallways, just enough to display decorative items such as small keepsakes, paintings and family photos.

AN & ERWAN BOUROULLEC DESIGN

EMMEMOBILI

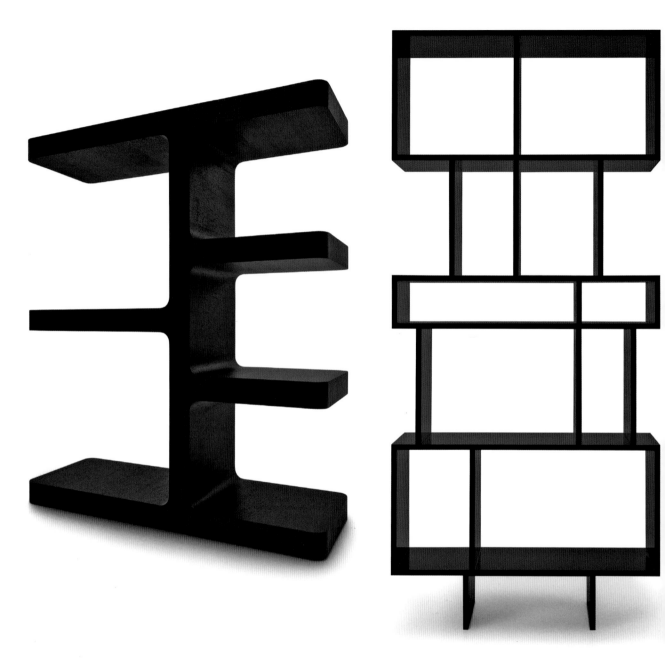

EMMEMOBILI

EMMEMOBILI

LAURA MERONI

>>104

Circular cabinets are perfect for the awkward corners in a home. Corner units appear small from the outside, but they actually have a large storage capacity.

DRIADE

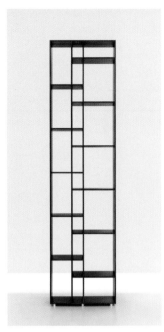

ZEITRAUM

ROBERTA EUSEBIO

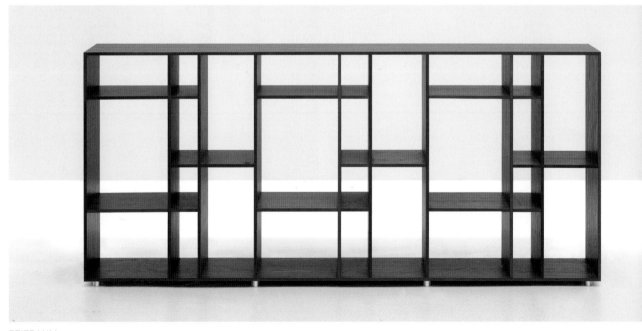

ZEITRAUM

>> **105** When decorating entrances, bear in mind that they can be very useful spaces. Therefore, try to find narrow furniture that is suitable for storing small to medium-sized objects.

RONAN & ERWAN BOUROULLEC DESIGN

XAM

NOVO

SICEA

OTTI

ADE

E15

MINOTTI

>> 106 A simple way to make hallways and badly lit corners stand out is to use light and colorful accessories.

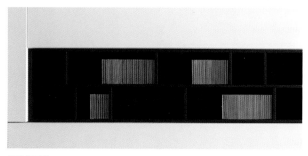

MINOTTI

DOMODINAMICA

DOIMO

SINTESI

MINOTTI

ESI

CCT

PORADA

NOVO

107

There are a wide range of stylish and clever coat racks and hooks available, which can be used as a decorative element while keeping coats, hats and scarves tidy. Hallways are the perfect location for occasional furniture.

NOVO

BATHROOMS

BUR

BATHROOMS

Throughout the 20th century, the room designed for the lavatory has become a space for both personal hygiene and health. This is reflected in the evolution of its elements, both their forms and their functions. Freestanding washbasins have been replaced with counters and sinks, bathtubs are integrated into units with a shower and there are lines of shelves and cabinets in which to store an abundance of tubes, creams, jars and bottles. The bathroom is our haven for our new-found devotion to our body.

108

In this bathroom, the storage consists of a wooden structure that is at the same height as the bathtub, so it can also be used as a bench. This also visually lightens the space.

© Mariana R. Eguaras Etc

Using boxes or baskets for storing the products and other personal belongings of each family member helps to maintain order on shelves and countertops. This leaves them accessible and makes it easier to clean these surfaces.

109

DURAVIT

465

110

When the aim is to accentuate the lightness of the space, a good option is either floating cabinets or a unit on wheels. Here, the light color of the furniture and the abundance of light are also key elements.

DURAVIT

111

Maximize your bathroom walls: here, the vanity, towel racks and recesses in the walls are creative solutions that produce a clean, simple space. The color adds a personal touch.

ROCA

The countertop of the vanity is the perfect surface on which to keep soaps, toothbrushes and other personal products. If the counter is not very big, only a single sink should be installed, in order to enhance the sense of spaciousness.

112

DINI

113 Mirrored cabinets provide a bathroom essential — a mirror — as well as discreet storage without detracting from the room's feeling of space.

A large basket for dirty laundry, which can be stored beneath a cabinet or the sink, is the key to a tidy bathroom. No matter how busy the home's residents are, the bathroom is left spotless after a quick shower or freshening up in the morning.

114

LAU

FEN

LAUFEN

DURAVIT

TOSCOQUA

115

The compact and lightweight feeling of this space is accentuated by the rectangular cabinets suspended above the floor, which have a large storage capacity. The glass front of the tall cabinet lightens the severity of its volume.

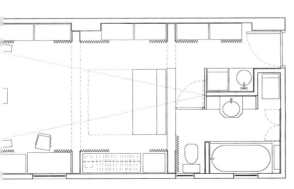

116

Custom-built furniture makes maximum use of every corner. Cabinets of sufficient depth can be designed to perfectly adapt to the style of the home and the available area, without cluttering the space.

117

A ledge on or beside a low window at the height of the countertop, serves as useful additional space, such as in this long and narrow bathroom. A narrow cabinet on the back wall harmonizes the furnishings.

STR

AVIT

118

A unit on wheels is the best choice if you decide on a countertop without a vanity. Here, the ledge beside the high window provides a surface on which to store extra towels or other objects.

119

A tall, narrow cabinet that extends to the ceiling provides sufficient storage space in smaller bathrooms. There is also the option of leaving the front uncovered to lighten the piece or using mirrors to visually increase the space.

120 The built-in cabinet on the wall and the recess with a shelf located in the hallway offer storage solutions for the small second bathroom, which lacks space for furniture or shelves.

121

Sometimes the simplest solution is the best way to ensure a sophisticated result. A simple square cabinet harmonizes the design of the sink, the location of the mirrors and the finish of the furniture.

BURGBAD

TOSCOQUAT

ACQUATTRO

122

A system of fixed cabinets and shelves decorate the entrance to this bathroom, providing the necessary space for storing small items not offered by the two slabs of stone used to build the base for the sink.

AGAPE

VIT

123

Though the storage needs of a bathroom are not excessive, the storage must be planned well to avoid conveying a sense of chaos. A single bank of cabinets can satisfy storage needs, but it has to be chosen carefully so that the size and the style adapt to the space.

124

The toilet and sink can be visually
separated by using a low wall
or by placing a pair of cabinets
perpendicular to the wall.

125

One option is to hide the bathroom fixtures and separate the shower and bathtub area without completely isolating the spaces. Transparent or frosted glass partitions are perfect for this purpose, as they separate the areas without visually reducing the size of the room.

A mirrored wall that conceals cabinets and plumbing and a custom towel rack installed behind the door: two solutions that can be combined to gain even more space.

126

Wall cabinets are the best solut storing your personal items. Generally come in small sizes and excessive c depth is not required. There is an a solutions to suit all budgets and all t

127

There are various options when fitting a basic storage space underneath the sink: a custom-made counter that takes up the full length of the wall, a simple shelf or a small vanity.

BURGBAD

Small and versatile pieces of furniture are best used in furnishing a small bathroom. It is important that the pieces are not too big so they do not obstruct movement or clutter the space.

128

BATHROOM FURNITURE

AXIA

BURGBAD

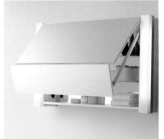

BURGBAD

>> **129** Fabric baskets or trays with compartments in the drawer of bathroom furniture keep everything neat and tidy, and objects will also be easier to

IKEA

DURAVIT

ANTONIO LUPI

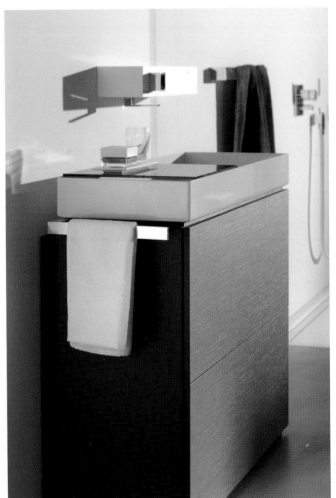

>>130 In many homes, hand towels can be hung on a towel rack integrated into the vanity. This will leave space on the walls for large bath towels.

ALAPE

HARDY INSIDE

BAD

BURGBAD

E15

>> 131

Creating a functional bathroom with many different types of organizers is the best way to keep smaller objects in order. Remember to keep medicine away from humid areas.

ALAPE

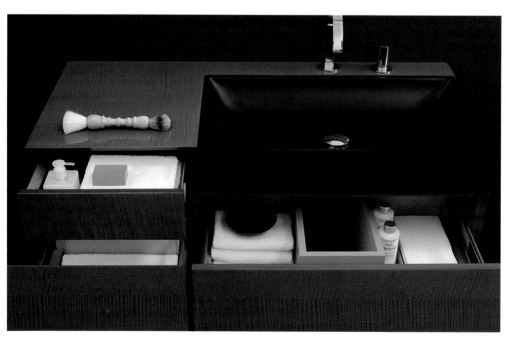

REGIA

INBANI

IKEA

>> 132 Whether out of habit or to save space, cabinets are traditionally placed against walls. However, if the bathroom is big enough, they can be used to divide spaces.

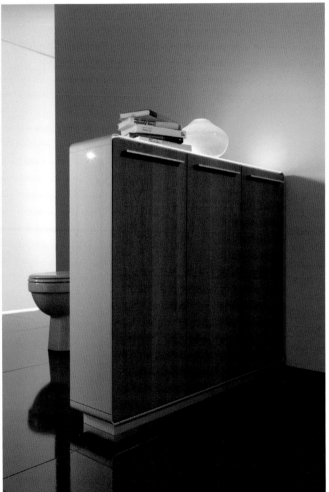

DURAVIT

MODÀ

DURAVIT

INBANI

IVANO RADAELLI

INBANI

AGAPE

Consistency in style helps to maintain a sense of order. It is therefore recommended that the same color and material are used for the wall units and the base of the vanity.

KOHLER

SMALLBONE OF DEVIZES

Install mirrored wall cabinets where they can be accessed easily and offer a good view of the contents inside, and reserve high wall cabinets for items that are used much less frequently.

AGAPE

ADA

HABITAT

AGAPE

WETSTYLE

DY INSIDE

POM D´OR

PE

MODÀ

LAV

LAUFEN

>>135 Organizing beauty and grooming essentials is a priority if you want an immaculate bathroom. For convenience and to save time, store products used on a daily basis in baskets or in the vanity.

CERAMICA CIELO

MUJI

AGAPE

GESSI

DURAVIT

POM D´OR

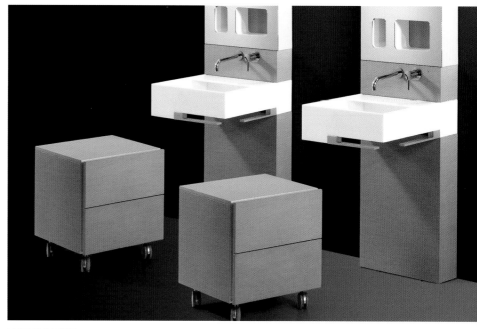

HARDY INSIDE

LAUFEN

RICHARD LAMPERT

NI

BURGBAD

AGAPE

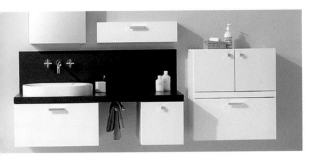

>>**136** Make use of pillars, setbacks and sloping ceilings for custom-made shelves. There is often space under a window for a small shelf or towel rack or a combination of both.

COGLIATI

LER

ZEITRAUM

TAT

HABITAT

WOODNOTES

IKEA

HABITAT

>>137 Towel racks should be located in obvious places, not only because it is necessary to have towels within reach, but also because they can be a major decorative element, particularly when the colors match those of the bathroom's design.

CA

KOHLER

MUJI

MUJI

MUJI

MUJI

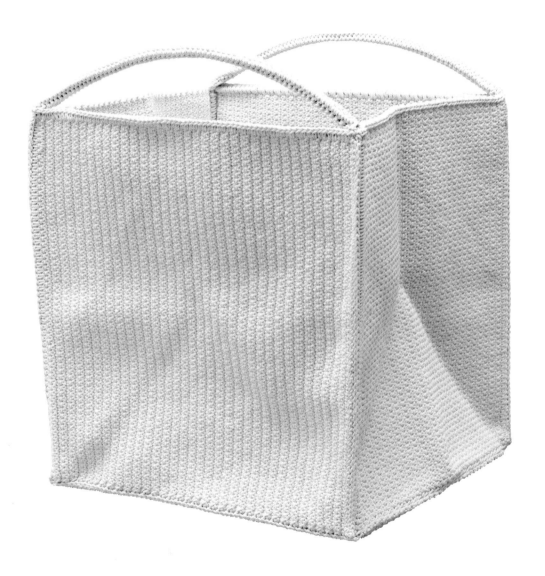

IKEA

>> **138** To bring order to the bathroom, use a combination of boxes and containers. It is a good idea to separate beauty products and creams by category: face, hair, body, mouth, etc.

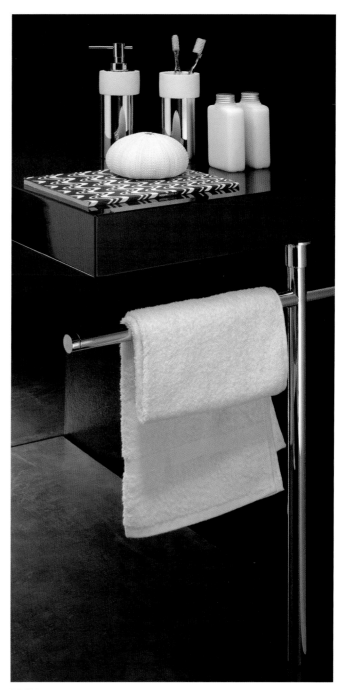

REGIA

WETSTYLE

HABITAT

HABITAT

MUJI

HABITAT

THG PARIS

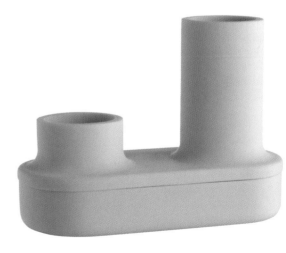

IKEA

LIVING AND DINING ROOMS

ZANC

LIVING AND DINING ROOMS

A place to meet and chat, a work space, a reading room, a TV room — all these features make the living room a multipurpose space where modern interior design can become blurred and more relaxed. It is an open room that sometimes can be combined with hallways, the kitchen, the dining room or the home office. When separated by movable panels or independent units, the spaces can be linked in a single area, where the decoration, along with versatile and imaginative storage, can be adapted to suit different needs. Standard storage elements in living and dining rooms are shelves and bookcases, sideboards, and units for audio and video equipment.

TENI

MOL

Sliding doors on a bookcase hide the contents from prying eyes, and these units can be used to store objects that are not used very often. If you wish to store collectibles or trinkets, glass doors allow the contents to be seen but protect them from dust.

139

ENI

140

This difficult architectural structure with sloping ceilings and columns, has been resolved by placing cabinets in the lowest areas of the ceilings and using the columns to frame a unit separating the two areas of the dining room.

141

Limited but well-chosen pieces of furniture are key to not obstructing movement and making a space seem bigger. Here, the glass table emphasizes this feature.

CATTELAN ITALIA

142

If you hide or camouflage audio equipment in a piece of furniture or a bookcase, take into account that a back exit for cables is required, as well as a space of at least 5 inches (12 cm) around and behind the device to ensure proper ventilation.

Història
La historia i l'agricultura

RAFEM

EMAR

143

Occasional furniture on which you place decorative items, such as books or small boxes, completely define the space. Next to a chair they create a reading corner, and in a hallway they can be used to display objects.

144

A low unit that runs along one wall near the sofa will provide endless storage possibilities and will not take up too much space. Painting it the same color as the walls will intensify this feeling and is a practical way to make the room feel more spacious.

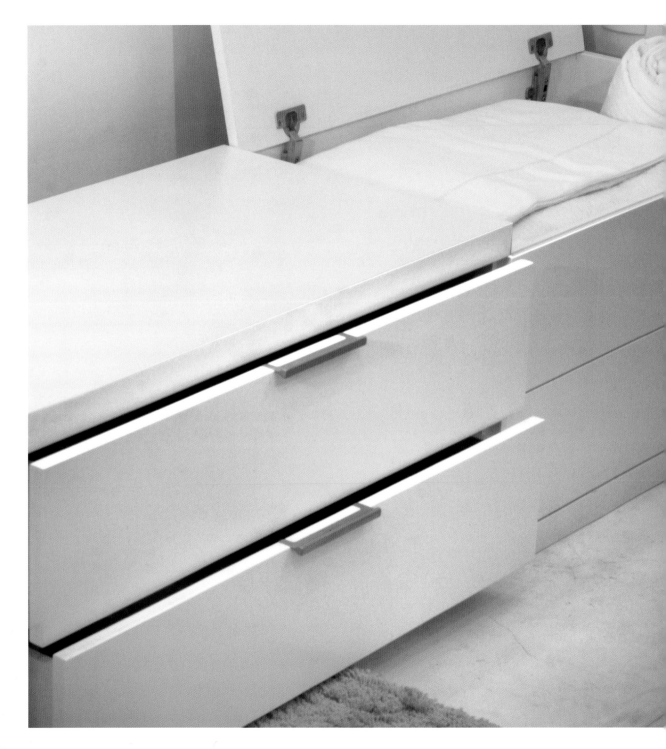

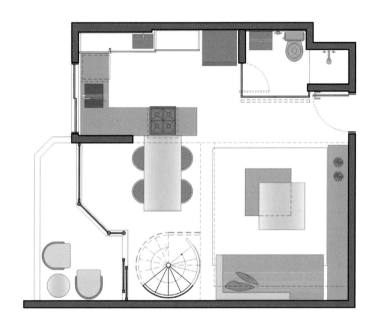

145

The lack of furniture adds light to this living room and helps to achieve an airy and relaxed atmosphere, but it is not always possible to make so little use of space. Here, the freestanding shelves are a lightweight solution.

The furniture and wall units provide
multiple storage options in this space.
The designer played with shapes, strong
colors and materials to create powerful,
imaginative, personal and decorative
solutions that offer the practicality of
cabinets and drawers.

146

LTO

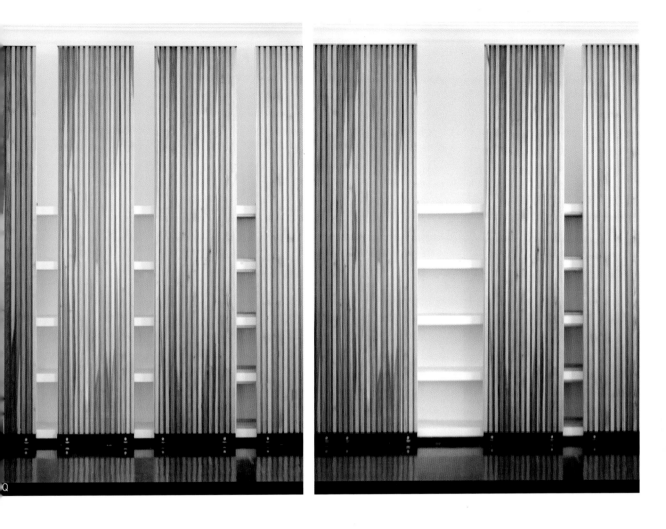

147

A wall with custom-made shelves is practical and changeable. Panels made from a contrasting material are used to cover and uncover the area. This play of movement creates a chameleonlike and dynamic space.

MORQ

RAFEMAR

RAFE

EMAR

148

If there is enough space, separate areas with bookcases or other medium-sized units to make the room seem larger. Use units that extend to the ceiling if you require extra storage space.

MINOTTI

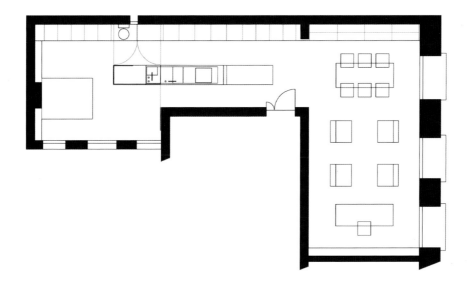

149

Two trends define the contemporary living-dining room: an open, transparent and undefined room with multifunctional and mobile furniture, and well-defined areas that are orderly, which is a more classical concept of space that provides specific solutions for every need and defines the use of every corner.

Storage units are required in any area where you read, watch television or listen to music. The variety of designs on the market means they can be also serve as decorative and practical elements.

150

ENI

ENI

CAS

Side tables integrated into the structure of the seats make good use of the back part of this sofa. Freestanding shelving on both sides reduces the amount of furniture needed and brings order to the space, as several functions are grouped into a single volume.

151

MOLT

A sideboard must have at least
one or two drawers for storing
flatware; a pair of large racks for
plates, platters and serving bowls;
a rack for glassware; and a space
for tablecloths, napkins, etc.

152

TENI

In the dining area it is important
to have a place to store flatware
and dishes. Use one or more wall
cabinets, a low unit with doors and
drawers or a built-in closet hidden
behind doors painted the same
color as the walls.

153

MOL

Store everything in a large bookcase that takes full advantage of the height of the room. It will be visually lighter if it frames a door or window.

154

MOL

ENI

155

Bookcases can have a major impact on the feel of a room; choose the size and placement carefully.

MOL

A television unit that hides the home theater system and corresponding cables brings order to the space. Drawers in which to store movies and games are ideal.

156

CARBE

157 Mobile and multifunctional pieces of furniture are one of the characteristics of contemporary living rooms, which are open spaces that need to be adapted to different requirements.

158 Custom-made furniture can adapt to irregular building structures and maximize storage space in awkward areas.

A small bookcase or a few
shelves under a window create
a discreet storage space, and
a ledge can be used as a work
surface or as a side table.

159

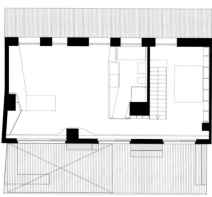

OTTA

C+I HAUS

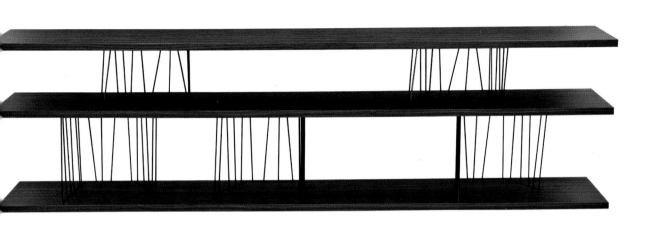

FLAI

>> # 160

Variation of color and shape can turn bookcases into decorative features. The right decision will solve storage problems but will also, and more importantly, decorate the room.

CASAMANIA

DOMODINAMICA

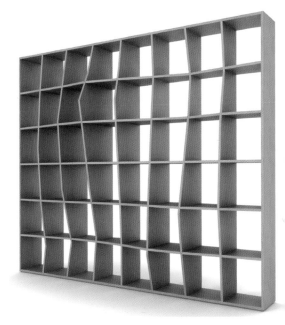

EMMEMOBILI

PRESOTTO

LAGO

BONALDO

>>161 Vertical structures add an extra dose of dynamism to a room. Whether they reach the ceiling or only halfway, bookcases such as these are ideal for small spaces or as secondary units in spacious rooms with several pieces of furniture.

ETIPO

NE

B-LINE

LAGO

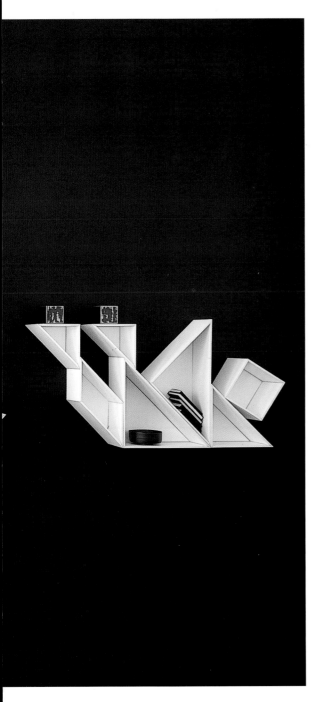

PORRO

BONALDO

AN & ERWAN BOUROULLEC DESIGN

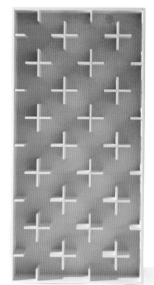

ARKETIPO

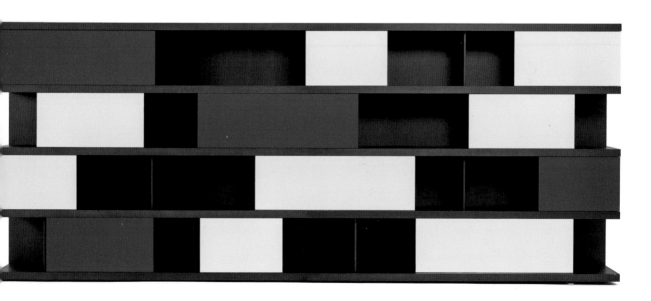

EMOBILI

>> 162 The lightness of today's storage units and bookcases marks the contemporary aesthetics of modern rooms. Original creations lacking in a central body that cut across the shelves can generate a lot of different forms with the books and articles stored inside.

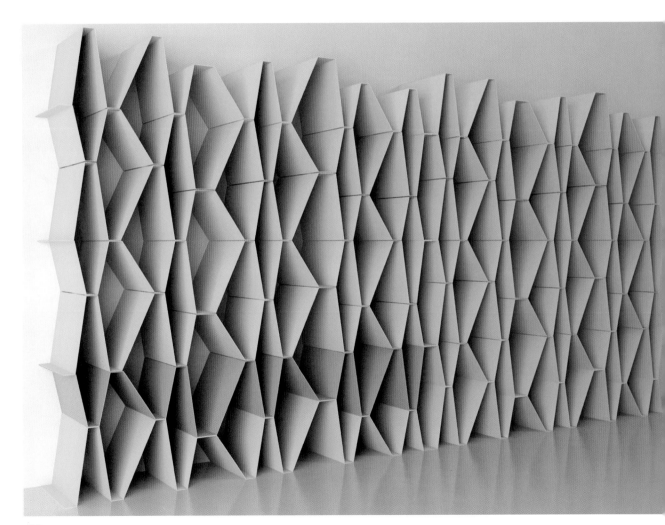

ITF

MANN-COPENHAGEN

LEONHARD PFEIFER

ZE & MILAN

RÖ

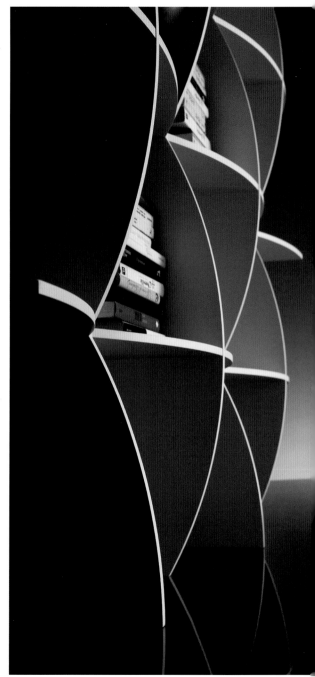

TRABALDO

SAKURA ADACHI

ZANOTTA

>> 163

Modular shelves' capacity to be transformed with sliding doors helps keep everything neat. Hidden compartments can store paperwork or toys and keep them out of sight.

ERI

PRESOTTO

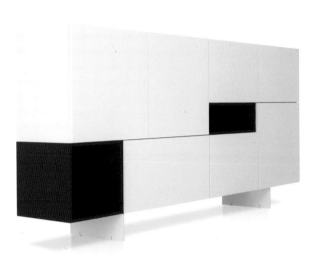

PORRO

CA

MODÀ

IKER

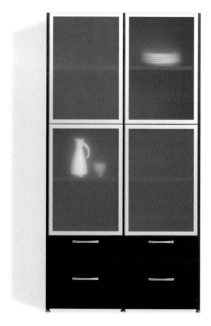

BO CONCEPT

1920

CECCOTTI

TIS

CASAMILANO

Adapted to the style of the room, sideboards provide very welcome storage space for tableware, flatware, paperwork, photo albums, etc. They are also a useful additional surface.

EMOBILI

MILANO

CASAMANIA

CREAZIONI

>>165

Although many believe sideboards are a little outdated and take up too much space, this is not the case. In fact, today's major furniture manufacturers offer these pieces in their most modern and daring designs.

CAPELLINI

VARASCHIN

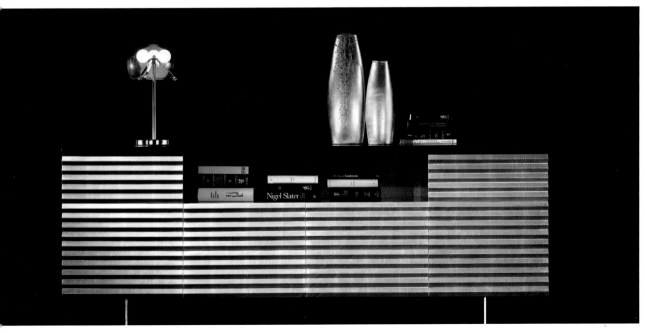

CASAMANIA

DOIMO

XAM

ADA

ADA

PIANCA

BO CONCEPT

ARKETIPO

DOIMO

BLÅ STATION

>>166

Side tables can be placed in hallways, corners or near the sofa. They also come in sets of two or three nested tables that can be stored one above the other and used when extra surfaces are required.

NELLI

MINOTTI

BO CONCEPT

FLAI

TJOHANSEN

BONALDO

Magazines and books can make a home look messy. To keep them within reach, hanging a pouch from the sofa is a good solution. When there is too much reading material, they can be stacked against the wall and used as a decoration.

STATION

BAULINE

>>168 Simplicity and functionality are high on the list of priorities in contemporary homes. Therefore, extendable tables are a good choice because they save space and keep the area clear.

.INE

.INE

CASAMILANO

COVO

B-LINE

PORRO

PIANCA

MATROSHKA

>>169 A great way to save space is to use versatile furniture that can be transformed and has several uses, such as a sofa with a back that converts into a small bar or an ottoman with storage space inside.

MILANO BEDDING

RÖ

MILANO BEDDING

NO BEDDING

NO BEDDING

LIGNE ROSET

OUTDOOR
SPACES

© Ricardo Labo

OUTDOOR SPACES

Furniture and architecture are key elements to consider when organizing outdoor spaces. Multifunctional pieces, such as teak or fiber boxes, can be used for storage and as tables or benches. Differences in levels or structures can form benches and tables, and are an ideal way to create storage compartments in which to keep all kinds of items, from garden tools to folding chairs.

An intelligent distribution of space helps to maintain order. Partition walls, strategically placed platforms and arbors are the foundation of a good use of exterior space.

ontse Garriga

170

If storage furniture is not taller than the deck's railings or walls, it can be located anywhere in the outdoor area without interfering with the order and distribution of the space's volumes.

171

A good way to keep spaces looking tidy is by selecting furniture that fits well together. When not in use, sun loungers with wheels can easily be moved and placed under the table.

In small spaces, an intelligent layout of the outdoor furniture will help you do away with unnecessary furniture. Differences in levels or gaps in the deck can become comfortable benches that are integrated into the architectural structure of the home.

172

Just like in the interior rooms of
a home, for maximum comfort on
a deck, terrace or other outdoos
area, furniture cannot occupy
more than one third of the space,
leaving at least two-thirds free.
This keeps the space from looking
cluttered and contributes to an
easier flow of movement.

173

A single divided structure can accommodate several different functions, which has the advantage of keeping the focus on a single main body. For example, in two perpendicular strips of cement a seating area, a garden and a fountain coexist harmoniously.

174

175

Garden boxes and pots in a row are a great way to maintain order in outdoor spaces. An arbor or gazebo is always an excellent way to provide shade and support for climbing plants.

176 Pergolas and decks are excellent ways to create sections within a large exterior space. The key to maintaining the visual order lies in not going beyond the limits of these defined spaces, within which you can place all the furniture and accessories.

To enhance the sense of relaxation while still keeping the outdoor area looking tidy, tie a hammock to two strong points of the walls, which will keep the ground visually clear.

177

178

A service area next to a pool can be concentrated into a single structure that contains a cooking area and showers. A shelf near the barbecue should store a big box in which to conveniently keep firewood or bags of charcoal.

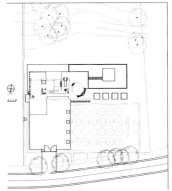

JAMES PLANT DESIGN

JAMES PLANT DESIGN

VITEO

179

When outdoor furniture is part of the same set with a shared design, color and style, it greatly contributes to the spaces sense of order. Better still if they are striking pieces without excessive ornaments or accessories.

SCHIN

1920

GANDIA BLASCO

PUNTMOBLES

LIGNE ROSET

>> 180 Folding, extendable or
nesting tables are a good
option when you have a s▮
deck or patio. Once they a▮
no longer needed, they ca▮
stored easily, even indoor▮
without cluttering the spa▮

SMART BEDS

SMART BEDS

ERRAZZE

HABITAT

HABITAT

UROS VITAS

DRIADE

ROCHE BOBOIS

A BOX

KETTAL

RIVA 1920

RICHARD LAMPERT

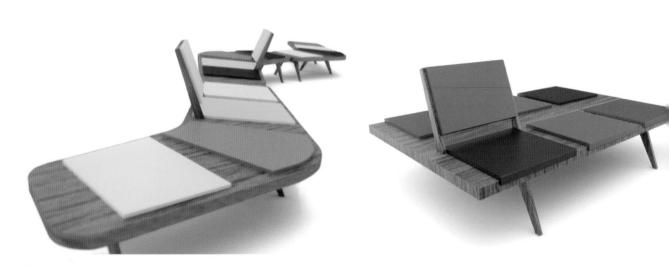

QUINZE & MILAN

ARUGA

>> 181

Gazebos create a meeting point in the yard and protect the furniture and accessories. If the gazebo is located far from the house, it should include a small storage cabinet for glasses, plates and basic utensils.

KETTAL

ARUGA

JANE HAMLEY WELLS

KETTAL

DEESAWAT

SUTHERLAND

AL

GANDIA BLASCO

TARTARUGA

BONACINA PIERANTONIO

722

ECCT

>>182 Furniture made of wicker or rattan, among other fibers, has different tones due to the fiber's texture. These pieces of furniture should be stored under cover, as the sun dries them out and water damages them. Their advantage is that they mix well with wrought iron furniture and with light and dark wood.

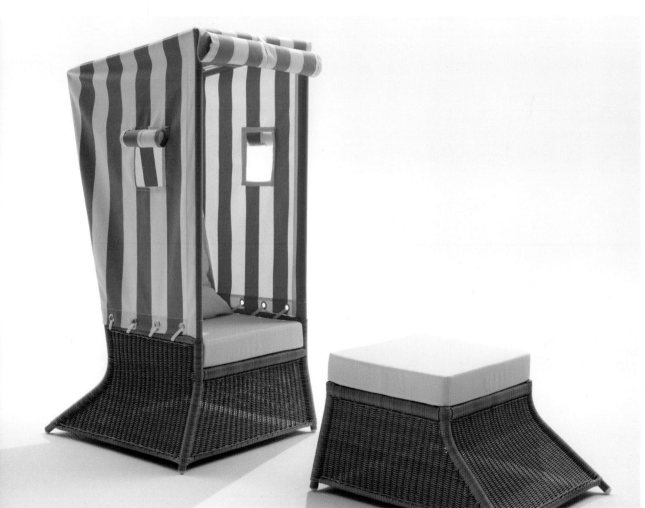

ACINA PIERANTONIO

KETTAL

TAL

TARTARUGA

TARUGA

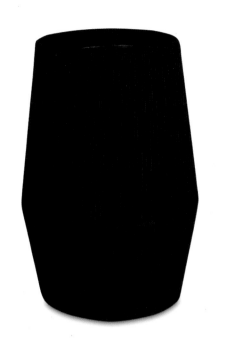

KETTAL

KETTAL

LE TERRAZZE

>> 183 Teak chests are very useful for storing cushions, lamps, candles and other objects. They can also be used as seating or as a side table.

HABITAT

LE TERRAZZE

SE

E15

°0

JANE HAMLEY WELLS

DEESAWAT

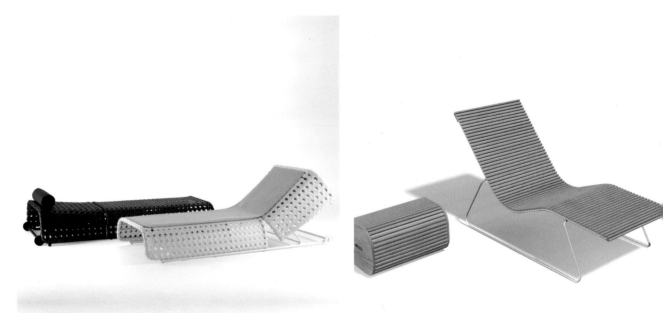

B&B ITALIA

ELITE

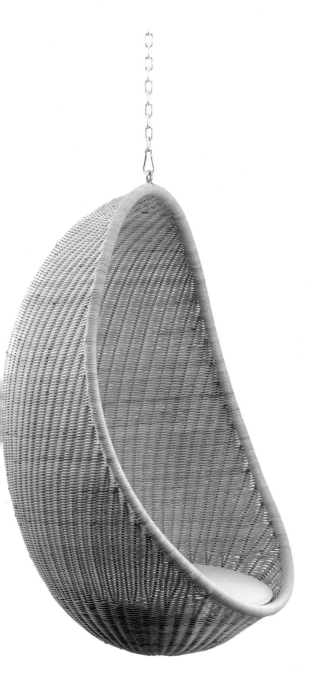

GANDIA BLASCO

DIA BLASCO

GANDIA BLASCO

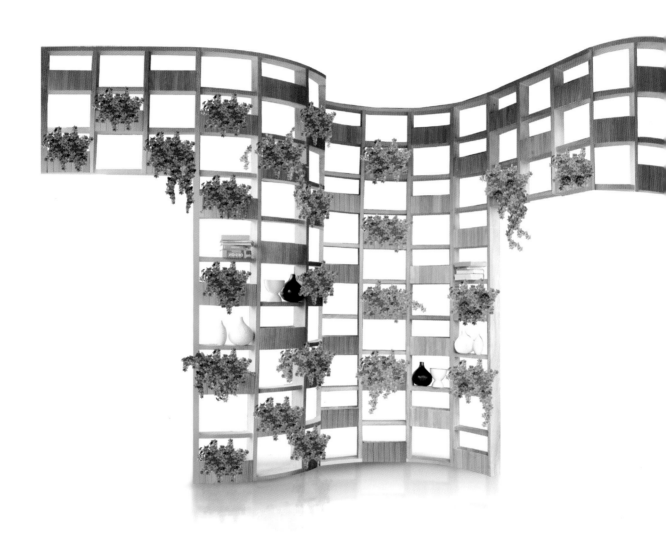

DEESAWAT

An ideal way to keep firewood tidy is the space underneath a modern, compact barbecue made of a lightweight material.

ITALIA

ALMA ASSOCIATI

CONMOTO

SUTHERLAND

SUTHERLAND

>>185

Cushions and ottomans are the best accessories to bring order to the backyard. When they are not used, they can be easily stacked in the garage.

NOVO

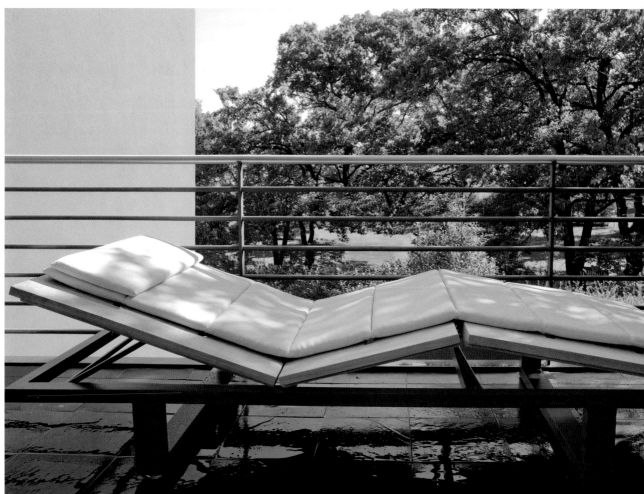

SUTHERLAND

ARUGA

FUN ROOMS

© Martyn O`Kelly/Redcover

FUN ROOMS

Today's stressful and hectic lifestyle takes its toll on both body and mind, and sometimes all we feel like doing is retreating into the comfort of our home so we can relax and escape from the responsibilities of life. In other words, we want to feel like a kid again. This chapter explores the idea of playrooms inside the home, particularly those geared to adults but also those that can be enjoyed by children as well. From high-tech gadgets and state-of-the-art equipment to table games and funky furniture, the selection of interiors this will inspire create their own fun room at home or simply offer a glimpse into the realm of home entertainment design.

186

An exotic interior design characterized by Asian references, intense colors and abstract paintings creates a sensuous and lively ambience fit for hosting gatherings, parties, and private screenings. A high-definition projector, sound system and screen allow for an integral viewing experience, while an exuberantly decorated bar provides an animated atmosphere for parties and get togethers.

In response to the client's request, the space was transformed into an intimate wine-tasting room and cellar with a glass portal-like entry. While preserving the exposed concrete, stone and wood ceilings, the designers invigorated the room with a bold red color, red floor cushions, wine racks and a tasting table.

187

188

Fitted with its own fireplace and leather armchairs, this room accommodates a large number of people, seating at least 10 at the bar. The space is animated by brightly colored walls, lively paintings and vintage posters and signs. The wine cellar features wine racks from Italy, a butcher's table from Hungary and small stools from a school in France.

189

This chill-out lounge was specifically designed to seat many people during relaxing movie sessions. Characterized by a stretch of low lounge seating, the space is dominated by a panoramic plasma screen and a curved central table with an integrated open fireplace.

190

A freestanding structure accommodates a wall unit with shelves for music equipment and other objects. The luxuries of a big-screen TV are enhanced by a built-in screen that can be pulled out from the partition structure to create a genuine home entertainment space.

191

The wall unit in this living area integrates a flat-screen TV and conceals a state-of-the-art sound system, providing an optimal viewing and listening experience for the residents and guests.

A pull-down screen concealed within the ceiling transforms the living area into a comfortable and intimate home theater.

192

193

The strategic placement of the screen allows the projected images to be viewed either from the living room or from an exterior deck on the upper level. The installation provides the opportunity for outdoor viewing sessions during the warmer months and creates an ideal environment for parties.

194

An easy and practical way to store dozens of DVDs is a made-to-measure bookcase with long, identical-sized shelves on which the movies can be organized alphabetically or by type.

195

A pool table, a drum set and large bean bag chairs make up this adult playroom, which offers a variety of activities for the owners and their guests to enjoy during their leisure time. The drums are placed on a circular pedestal to add a theatrical quality and allow the player to feel as if on a stage. A large shelf unit on the wall emphasizes the playful character of the room and provides space for decorative objects.

196

Plush bean bag chairs, velvety textures and curved forms are combined with 1960s and 1970s patterns and bright colors to create a lighthearted atmosphere that is entertaining for all the senses.

SALUC

MODÀ

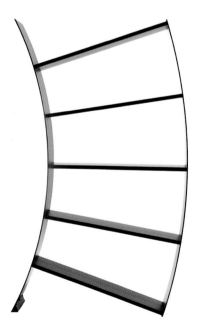

DRIADE

LEMA

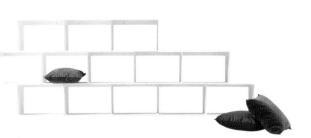

>>197 The arrangement of objects on shelves can add a decorative element, in particular to rooms that have been painted in one color. For example, only displaying objects on the middle shelves can create a stunning visual effect.

ITALIA

EMMEMOBILI

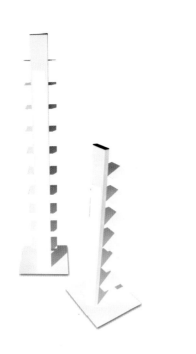

SAPIENS

SEVENSALOTTI

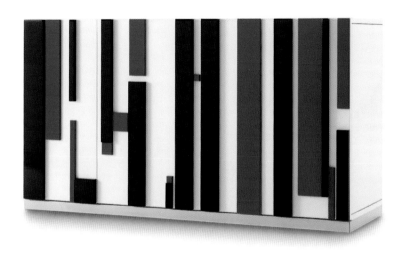

RÖ

DRIADE

EMMEMOBILE

EMMEMOBILE

FITTING

RÖ

If you do not have a basement in which to install a wine cellar, investing in special furniture is worthwhile. Some are designed to stack bottles in a decorative way. Others include spaces for glasses and accessories.

ESOTTO

ARFLEX

FLEX

MODÀ

YOMEI

775

>>199

Units that can hold the television, DVD player, computer, stereo, etc., can create a multimedia space in any location in the home without taking up too much room, and they prevent the disorder that electrical cables create.

MOLTENI

DOIMO

PRESOTTO

EMMEI

CAPELLINI

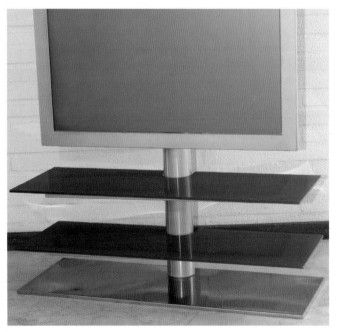

LA OCA

ROCHE BOBOIS

WEDGE

ROCHE BOBOIS

>>**200**

Magazines, movies, CDs and, in particular, remote controls are usually all over the place, creating a mess. Keep them together in a basket or, in central table with drawers or a special unit so they're within easy reach.

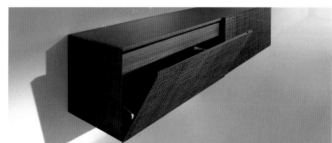

MEI

DICHIENTI

LAURA MERONI

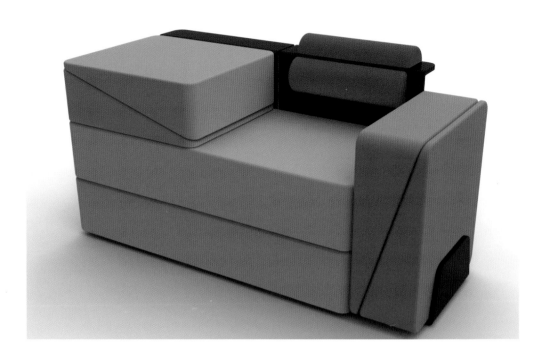

BRIGHTSIDE

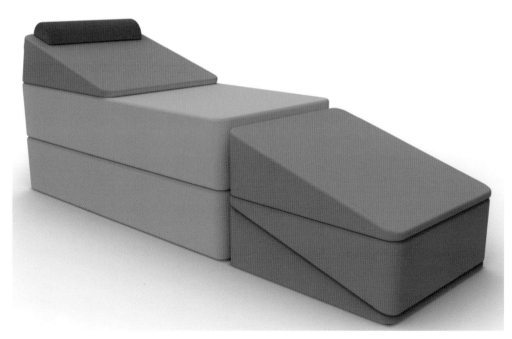

PRESOTTO

RONAN & EWAN BOUROULLEC DESIGN

TTUNO by ACERBIS

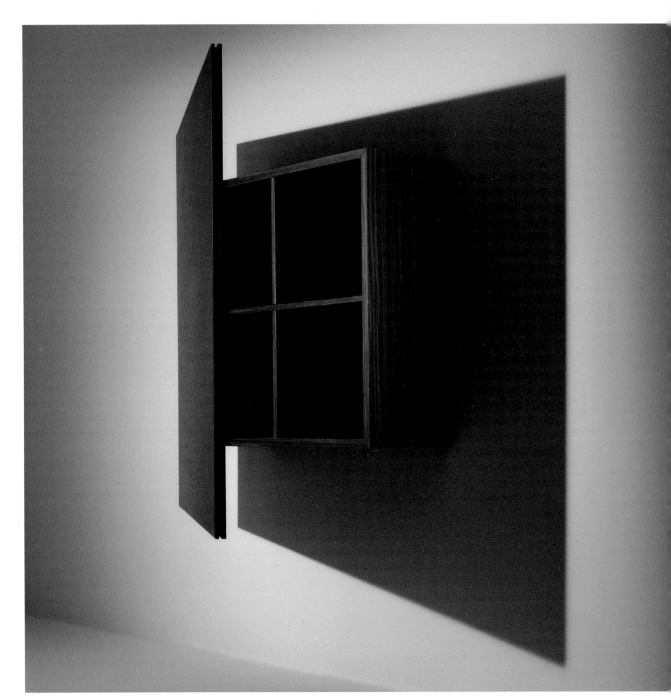

LAURA MERONI

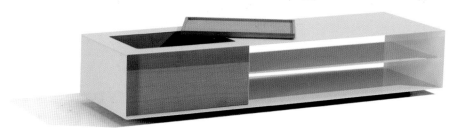

FELICE ROSSI

1MEMOBILI

LAURA MERONI

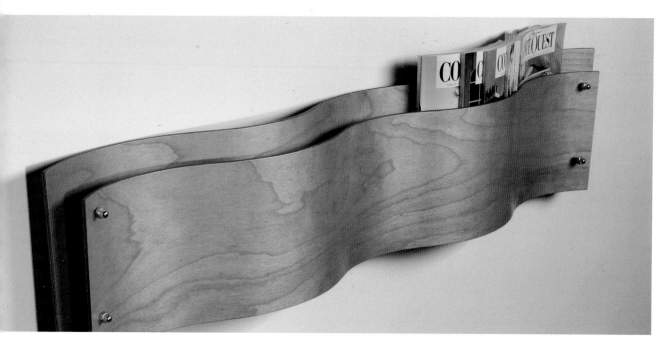

IKO SUKEGAWA

Emili Fox
Mosman, Australia
© Eric Sierens
p. 680

Estudio Cano Lasso
Madrid, Spain
www.canolasso.com
© Diego Cano, Ana Carvalho,
Pablo Zuloaga
p. 140

Fabrizio Leoni
Barcelona, Spain
www.fabrizioleoniarchitettura.com
© Dessi e Monari
pp. 57, 58

Fernandes Capanema Arquitetura
Brasilia, Brazil
www.fernandescapanema.com.br
© Marri Nogueira, Clausem Bonifacio
pp. 134, 135, 576, 578

Fernando Rihl/Procter-Rihl
London, United Kingdom
www.procter.rihl.com
© Fernando Rihl
pp. 19, 20, 21

Filippo Bombace Architetto
Rome, Italy
www.filippobombace.com
© Luigi Filetici
p. 432, 433

Finn & Hattie/Maine Cottage
Yarmouth, ME, U.S.
www.mainecottage.com
© Finn & Hattie/Maine Cottage
p. 300

Frank La Rivière
Tokyo, Japan
www.frank-la-riviere.com
© Ryota Atarashi, Shinkenchiku-sha
p. 410

Gary Chang/EDGE (HK) Ltd
Hong Kong, China
www.edge.hk.com
© Almond Chu
pp. 224, 482, 483, 484

Groep Delta Architectur
Hasselt, Belgium
© Groep Delta Architectur
pp. 700, 701

Grollmitz-Zappe
Berlin, Germany
www.grollmitz-zappe-architekten.de
© Kirsti Kriegel
pp. 510, 511, 512

Guillermo Arias & Luis Cuartas
Bogota, Colombia
www.octubre.com.co
© Eduardo Consuegra
pp. 408, 463
© Eduardo Consuegra, Pablo Rojas
p. 500
© Pablo Rojas, Álvaro Gutiérrez
pp. 28, 30

Heather Spencer Designs
Landcashire, United Kingdom
www.spencer.u-net.com
© Heather Spencer Designs
pp. 301, 302, 358

Helen Weals
Bocca de Styx, FL, U.S.
© Tyson Vacuum
pp. 114, 115, 424, 425

Hobby a. Schuster & Maul
Salzburg, Austria
www.hobby-a.at
© Marc Haader
p. 485

Hofman Dujardin Architecten
Amsterdam, Netherlands
www.hofmandujardin.nl
© Matthijs van Roon
p. 205

Horm
Azzano Decimo, Italy
www.horm.it
© Karim Rashid
p. 439

Jamie Loft
Melbourne, Australia
www.4blue.com.au
© Shania Shegedyn
p. 682

Jean Bocabeille & Ignacio Prego
Paris, France
© Ken Hayden/Redcover.com
p. 680

Jo Warman
London, United Kingdom
© Mike Daines/Redcover.com
p. 746

Jonathan Levi
Boston, MA, U.S.
www.leviarc.com
© Anton Grassl, Jonathan Levi
p. 36

Johnson Chou
Toronto, ON, Canada
www.johnsonchou.com
© Volker Seding Photography
pp. 502, 503, 504

Jorge Segarra Checa
Valencia, Spain
© Joan Roig
p. 752

Kabalab
Brooklyn, NY, U.S.
www.kabalab.com
© Kabalab
pp. 178, 179

Karim Rashid
New York, NY, U.S.
www.karimrashid.com
© Simon Upton/The Interior Archive
p. 760

Landau & Kindelbacher
Munich, Germany
www.landaukindelbacher.de
R&R Hackl, Landshut
p. 702

Lopez Rivera Architectes
Barcelona, Spain
© Jordi Miralles
p. 752

Lundberg Design
Napa, CA, U.S.
© César Rubio
p. 744

Malo Planning
Tokyo, Japan
www.malo.co.jp
pp. 136, 138, 411

Matt Gibson A+D
Sydney, Australia
www.mattgibson.com.au
© John Wheatley
p. 694

MB Studio–Sistema MIDI
Roda de Ter, Spain
www.sistema-midi.com
© MB Studio
pp. 202, 430, 507

Michael P. Johnson
Cave Creek, AZ, U.S.
www.mpjstudio.com
© Bill Timmerman
p. 430

Moriko Kira
Amsterdam, Netherlands
www.morikomira.nl
© Satoshi Asakawa
pp. 48, 49

Nico Rensch
London, United Kingdom
© Mark Luscombe-Whyte/The Interior Archive
p. 758

Oskar Leo Kaufmann
Dornbirn, Austria
www.olkruf.com
© Adolf Bereuter
pp. 14, 15

Pablo Fernández Lorenzo, Pablo Redondo Díez
Madrid, Spain
© Pablo Fernández Lorenzo, Pablo Redondo Díez
pp. 416, 417, 594

Page Goolrick Architect PC
New York, NY, U.S.
www.goolrick.com
© John M. Hall
pp. 196, 198

Périphériques Architectes
Paris, France
www.peripheriques-architectes.com
© H. Abadie
pp. 412, 413

Philippe Harden
Paris, France
www.philippeharden.com
© Philippe Harden
pp. 418, 419

Pont Reyes
Barcelona, Spain
© Gogortza & Llorella
p. 754, 756

Pugh & Scarpa Architects
Santa Monica, CA, U.S.
www.pugh-scarpa.com
© Pugh & Scarpa Architects
p. 429

Rafael Berkowitz/RB Architect
New York, NY, U.S.
www.rbarchitect.com
© James Wilkins
pp. 119, 572

René Chavanne
Vienna, Austria
www.renechavanne.com
© René Chavanne
pp. 38, 39

Resolution 4 Architecture
New York, NY, U.S.
www.re4a.com
© Esto Photography, Jeff Goldberg
p. 604

Salmela Architect
Duluth, MN, U.S.
www.salmelaarchitect.com
© Peter Bastianelli Kerze
p. 414

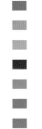

BRAND DIRECTORY

ACERBIS
www.acerbisinternational.com

AGAPE
www.agapedesign.it

ALAPE
www.alape.com

ANTONIO LUPI
www.antoniolupi.it

ARKETIPO
www.arketipo.com

ARFLEX
www.arflex.it

ARTIFICIO
www.artificio.es

ASSOMOBILI
www.assomobili.com

B&B ITALIA
www.bebitalia.it

B-LINE
www.b-line.it

BAULINE
www.bauline.it

BELLIGOTTI
www.belligotti.it

BERLONI CUCINE
www.berloni.it

BLÅ STATION
www.blastation.se

BO CONCEPT
www.boconcept.es

BOFFI
www.boffi.com

BONACINA PIERANTONIO
www.bonacinapierantonio.it

BONALDO
www.bonaldo.it

BULTHAUP
www.bulthaup.com

BURGBAD
www.burgbad.com

BUSNELLI
www.busnelli.it

CALLIGARIS
www.calligaris.it

CAMPEGGI
www.campeggisrl.it

CAPELLINI
www.cappellini.it

CASAMANIA
www.casamania.it

CASAMILANO
www.casamilanohome.com

CASSINA
www.cassina.it

CATTELAN ITALIA
www.cattelanitalia.com

CECCOTTI
www.ceccotticollezioni.it

CERAMICA CIELO
www.ceramicacielo.it

CESAR
www.cesar.it

CIA INTERNATIONAL
www.ciainternational.it

COCO MAT
www.coco-mat.com

COGLIATI
www.cogliati-cogliati.it

CONMOTO
www.conmoto.com

COVO
www.covo.it

CREAZIONI
www.stile-creazioni.com

DADA
www.dadaweb.it

DEAR KIDS
www.dearkids.it

ECOLAV
www.decolav.com

DEESAWAT
www.deesawat.com

DI LIDDO & PEREGO
www.diliddoeperego.it

DI PALMA ASSOCIATI
www.dipalmassociati.com

DESALTO
www.desalto.it

DRIADE
www.driade.com

DO+CE
www.do-ce.com

DOIMO
www.doimo.it

DOMODINAMICA
www.domodinamica.com

DUFFY LONDON
www.duffylondon.com

DURAVIT
www.duravit.es

E15
www.e15.com

ELMAR CUCINE
www.elmarcucine.com

EMMEBI
www.emmebidesign.com

EMMEI
www.emmei.it

EMMEMOBILI
www.emmemobili.it

ENGEL BRECHTS
www.engelbrechts.com

ERBA MOBILI
www.erbamobili.it

ERNESTO MEDA
www.ernestomeda.es

FELICE ROSSI
www.felicerossi.it

FITTING
www.fittingfitting.it

FISHBOL
www.fishbol.org

FLAI
www.flaiweb.it

FLOU
www.flou.it

FORMER
www.former.it

FRATELLI SPINELLI
www.fratellispinelli.it

GALOTTI & RADICE
www.gallottiradice.it

GANDIA BLASCO
www.gandiablasco.com

GESSI
www.gessi.com

GIORGETTI
www.giorgetti-spa.it

GRUPPO EUROMOBIL
www.euromobil.it

HABITAT
www.habitat.net

HARDY INSIDE
www.hardyinside.com

HORM
www.horm.it

IKEA
www.ikea.com

IMA MOBILI
www.ima-mobili.com

INBANI
www.inbani.com

IVANO RADAELLI
www.ivanoredaelli.it

JAMES PLANT DESIGN
www.jamesplantdesign.com

JANE HAMLEY WELLS
www.janehamleywells.com

JESSE
www.jesse.it

KABALAB
www.kabalab.com

KETTAL
www.kettal.es

KOHLER
www.kohler.com

LA OCA
www.laoca.com

LAGO
www.lago.it

LAMMHULTS
www.lammhults.se

LAUFEN
www.laufen.com

LAURA MERONI
www.laurameroni.com

LE TERRAZZE
www.pircher.eu

LEMA
www.lemamobili.com

LEONHARD PFEIFER
http://pfeifer.squarespace.com

LIGNE ROSET
www.ligne-roset.com

MDF ITALIA
www.mdfitalia.it

MAGIS
www.magisdesign.com

MAGNUS LONG
www.magnuslong.com

MAPINI
www.mapini.com

MATROSHKA
www.matroshka.se

MICUNA
www.micuna.com

MILANO BEDDING
www.milanobedding.it

MINOTTI
www.minotti.com

MISO SOUP DESIGN
www.misosoupdesign.com

MOBALCO
www.mobalco.com

MOBLES 114
www.mobles114.com

MODÀ
www.modacollection.it

MOLTENI
www.molteni.it

MONTIS
www.montis.nl

MOROSO
www.moroso.it

MORQ
www.morq.it

MOVE
www.move.it

MUJI
www.muji.com

MUEBLES BENICARLÓ
www.mueblesbenicarlo.com

NORMANN-COPENHAGEN
normann-copenhagen.com

NOVO
www.novoitalia.it

NUEVA LÍNEA
www.nuevalinea.es

O&G
www.olivoegodeassi.it

OFFECCT
www.offecct.se

OLIVIERI
www.olivierimobili.com

O.T.S. SELLEX
www.sellex.es

PEDINI
www.pedini.it

PIANCA
www.pianca.it

P'KOLINO
www.pkolino.com

POM D´OR
www.pomdor.com

PORADA
www.porada.it

PORCELANOSA
www.porcelanosa.com

PORRO
www.porro.com

PRESOTTO
www.presottoindustriemobili.com

PUNTMOBLES
www.puntmobles.com

QUINZE & MILAN
www2.quinzeandmilan.tv

RAFEMAR
www.rafemar.com

IONAL
w.rational-online.com

HARD LAMPERT
w.richard-lampert.de

A 1920
w.riva1920.it

BOTS
w.robots.it

CA
w.roca.com

CHE BOBOIS
w.roche-bobois.com

w.roethlisberger.ch

NAN & EWAN BOUROULLEC DESIGN
w.bouroullec.com

GIANO
w.rugiano.com

KURA ADACHI
w.sakurah.net

LUC
w.saluc.com

NKTJOHANSER
w.hubertmatthiassanktjohanser.de

HIFFINI
w.schiffini.it

HMIDT
w.schmidt-cocinas.es

VENSALOTTI
w.sevensalotti.it

SICEA
www.siceagroup.it

SINTESI
www.gruppo-sintesi.com

SMALLBONE OF DEVIZES
www.smallbone.co.uk

SMART BEDS
www.colombo907.com

SOFA BOX
www.sofabox.ch

STRUCH
www.struch.es

SUB-ZERO WOLF
http://www.westye.eu.com

SUTHERLAND
www.sutherlandteak.com

TARTARUGA
www.pircher.eu

TECNOCUCINA
www.tecnocucina.com

TEKA
www.teka.es

THG PARIS
www.thg.fr

TOSCOQUATTRO
www.toscoquattro.it

TRABALDO
www.trabaldosrl.com

TUTTUNO
www.acerbisinternational.com

UROS VITAS
universityofbelgrade.blogspot.com

VALCUCINE
www.valcucine.it

VALDICHIENTI
www.valdichienti.it

VARASCHIN
www.varaschin.it

VICCARBE
www.viccarbe.com

VITEO
www.viteo.at

VITRA
www.vitra.com

WEDGE
www.wedge.ie

WETSTYLE
www.wetstyle.ca

WOGG
www.wogg.ch

WOODNOTES
www.woodnotes.fi

XAM
www.xam.it

YOMEI
www.yomei.de

ZANOTTA
www.zanotta.it

ZEITRAUM
www.zeitraum-moebel.de